Lucky Shadows

Lucky Shadows

the selected poems of
Peter Lamborn Wilson

cover by James Koehnline

2018

Xexoxial Editions
West Lima, Wisconsin

ISBN-10: 1-936687-43-7
ISBN-13: 978-1-936687-43-5

Acknowledgements

Most of the poems are previously unpublised but read by PLW *viva voce* and recorded by Chris Funkhouser for PennSound (*http://writing.upenn.edu/pennsound*). Thanks also to Charles Bernstein and Al Filreis.

For editing all poems thanks to Raymond Foye and Charles Stein.

Some poems appeared in *Metambesen*, edited by Robert Kelly and Charlotte Mandel.

A companion volume to this one titled *Vanished Signs*, has been published by Lunar Chandelier Collective. (Thanks to Tamas Panitz and Lila Dunlop.)

published by

Xexoxial Editions
10375 County Highway Alphabet
La Farge, Wisconsin
54639

www.xexoxial.org
perspicacity@xexoxial.org

for
Ed & Miriam

Pound a hawk's egg with myrrh
put it on your eyes
you will see LUCKY SHADOWS
head & blood of a hoopoe
paint your eyes
then you will see them

—from *The Leyden Papyrus:
An Egyptian Magical Book*
(London, 1904)

Ghazals

GHAZAL IN "N"

Knots tied & breathed on somewhere when
in the desert under the proper moon

always leave some fruit behind like spoor
pomegranate blood orange mangosteen

I raised the wind but it blew back in my face
burnt my harvest ten-year wages of sin

summer afternoon: meander: cellar door
I never find you—a kind of anti-Zen

If I could leave myself to you in my will
I'd gladly consider death & resurrection

NON-GHAZAL

I want to tell you of my love
    but can find no hidden place
because all time & space is
    under surveillance

My data body is too big
    fatter than a thousand Afghans or Africans
and you are too small like a germ in the bloodstream
    to chase with any nano-submarine

through the empire of delight into
    the catastrophic basin of
whatever happens. Alas we failed
    to expropriate the Bank in 1870

you see the result
    the upshot the bottom line
sufism was once a reality without a name & now
    is a name without reality.

PSEUDO-GHAZAL

"Je ne regret rien"
—Edith Piaf

Decent reticence allows us not to name
you in this safe sufiistic allegory

poem as Dead Letter Office
Lost/Found Bureau of goodbyes

telephone line to heaven on high
long since disconnected for unpaid bills

True lovers desire Separation
mystical wine fermented from sour grapes

a stoic bolus that chokes us with gnostalgia
words as leeches for throbbing brows.

GHAZAL

You can't do a proper ghazal around a hole
    punched-out silhouette, disappearance

like rubaiyyat without the ruby. Something
    must persist if only lingering incense of absence

if only the lees, a headache in every sip.
    Arabs who've folded their tents & gone

leave behind traces, ashes
    of doused campfires, certain scents

of burnt-out desertification, hanging odes
    to a series of betrayals & abandonments.

TERRORIST GHAZAL

No such species as nightingale exists
    merely a few brokenhearted sparrows

exiled from cold nests & pierced
    with unnatural desire for a kind of scented cabbage.

We don't have them here in these austere &
    Protestant vales where their niche is filled by mockingbirds.

Of all arts theirs feels most terroristic
    most akin to the chemistry of a slow insidious bomb

music as pure resistance, expression devoid
        of all bourgeois striving for significance,
                for the merely sad.

GLOOMY GHAZAL

Fall in love w/ a goblin who distorts yr days
w/ unconsciousness of dusk & sorrow

let rain into the house of a daytime ghost
we're drifting off the grid—O Clouds

only pathetic wetlands w/ fallacious mist
& a hole where yr favorite spook will soon appear

photo of half-decayed house & old hag
in *Tri-Racial Isolates of the Jersey Pine Barrens*

shadow falls across mildewed page waiting
into the Hollow for the stars like nails

mail-order catalogs from the Atlantis League,
                                      up in the hills
where no one pays taxes, spending the day in bed,
                                      not doing their chores.

GHAZAL

the pen is in the hand of the witness
inscription of incense, alphabet of sylphs

nocturnal emissions & ectoplasmic codes
spell out Maktoub, it is written, Kismet

the platform of the railway station at Poughkeepsie
is the center of the universe

a face in the crowd disappears
in the moment of a timeless space

if only these angels knew their power
they could have all poets for their slaves

they could perch in my prayer niche any day
heathen idols served with silver paper & spice

but instead they slip away & leave no trace
the code uncracked, the manuscript erased.

GHAZAL FOR A LUNAR ECLIPSE

Tarnished w/ the cuprous leprosy of eclipse
the Moon of Alabama is the Moon of Afghanistan

but never the Moon of our uninsured senescence
always somewhere else exiled & displaced

we never stand under our own Moon
our militarized hallucinogenic real estate

but someone else's satellite, its tides
no longer stir our amniotic broth.

O Moon of alienation we now must say goodbye
we've lost our lunar shadow—the Dog in the Moon

still howling for the Moon, still beating
pots & pans to dispell the dark's invasion

O Moon of astronauts & dead bankers
our former homeland, our Zion.

NEO-GHAZAL

Running away to Baden-Baden
    to join the Cirque d'Hiver

the Caravan of Winter
    its delectable ennui

one becomes the enemy
    viz. Vienna's secret Ottoman Id,
            the COFFEE HOUSE

triste Trieste (Mad Carlotta, etc.)
    & finally San Francisco

leaving the air-conditioned ruins
    for some pocket of underdevelopment

where not everything has been replaced yet
    by its trembling hologram

Venice in February maybe
    the Seal of the Saints.

GHAZAL

Fermentation?
What's NOT in ferment?

Every quark is a yoghurt-producing bacterium
all atoms are yeast. Living bubbles

are oozing out of the interstices of
dry sepulchral dust
                              every moment

another last trump.
                              Siduri
"Bar Maid to the Gods" advises

Gilgamesh that beer is the lost
herb of immortality.
                              Raven

is the source of all champagne
as well as bread & thus

we picture him in a silk
smoking jacket &
                              red fez.

GHAZAL

This is the ghazal of the here & now &
not pale hands beside the Shalimar

How does it happen that the
poem of complaint is no longer possible

or that men have ceased in public to
weep & faint from sheer emotion

perhaps due to dietary deficiency &
sexual repression under early Capitalism

Opium of love & religion is transformed
into the Prozac of the Masses

sinks without trace into bathos like
mastodon in La Brea Tarpit

creepy as funeral jewelry. Only pariahs
still relish such unsavory seizures.

GHAZAL

& who am I, this mask that addresses you
but leaves no address—this message in a bottle?

In the scene where angry peasants with torches
storm the lightning-crown'd mad doctor's lab

screaming Down With Progress or Smash the Machines
I'm there in the mob, face hidden in a cowl

hunched & lumpen, shaking misshapen fist
w/ Epimethean rancor at the burning keep.

Bring back King Farouk or the imbecile Ottoman Caliph
for even graveyard dirt tastes better than antibiotics—

above all one misses their sheer ineptitude
laziness impurity superstition & other virtues

even the 19th century w/ all its horrors
its horses, its haschisch, its slanting sepia light.

GHAZAL

Form dictates content   the tearfulness
of calligraphy induces mournfulness

the alphabet itself a lacrimarium
that reeks of natron balsam & black crepe

October comes with its tales of the crypt
official seasonal opening of dim closing-in

text as revenant of orality's body
all writing is ghost-writing & thaumaturgy

We cherish the autumnal penumbra
that hovers round fading umber ink

leaf means page in every language
Eden's abecedarium fallen from Eve's apple

each sheet with its glyph & enigma
soon to be erased by irony or smoke.

GHAZAL

The nape of the neck of the just—
trimmed hair of the snow

its negative ionization its splash of
eau de cologne from the O-Zone

its frozen matriarchy w/ its hibernation
hypnosis & soft buried gnosis

its Japanese dialectic monotony—Prince Genji's
blue nose—Basho's numb toes

proposes an architecture w/out architects'
obtrusive egos & molds us

a universal igloo enclosing its own
exteriority—a Moebius House

or dance-hall for never-sober
animal spirits & would-be eskimos.

JOBS FOR HORSES

I await the first ox or horse
not breathlessly but impatiently

the first horse not ridden for hobby
first ox used because cheaper than tractor

pray I live to overhear the first
teenagers talking about fast horses

to see India in America—one-horse gigs
for rakish gents & bullocks for squares

Afghanistan in Upstate NY—shabby
Russian droshkys—Bactrian camels

plodding the verges of crumbling thru-ways
caravanserais under the clover-leaves

flatbreads & sheep entrails sold
from the shells of ruined McDonalds.

GHAZAL

Secrecy's an animal trait, every fox's burrow
& mole's lair a veritable Soviet bureau

Certain insect routines rival the KGB
but without paper, all done by ESP

the ultimate omerta—some birds you can tell
by their faces are paranoid as hell

and therefore art is justified, a kind of nest
where fertile eggs are held close to the vest

like aces up Houdini's sleeve or loves
that dare not speak their name, rabbits, doves

The rausch comes from what's never seen or said
Art's not the face but the skull in the head

It gains most power where it most conceals
& wins each trick each time it gets the deal.

GHAZAL

I've caught a disease called poetry
but lucky for you it's not communicable

I feel myself becoming marquis or
count palatine, schizo-grifter

self-conned, auto-magnetized, muse-
or monkey-ridden. Drunk on gardenias

swell in tails & topper, carriage ride
for one in Central Park by moon

strewing these reams of leaves of
grass like counterfeit two-dollar bills

my rank is raised. I weigh myself
in diamonds for distribution to the faithless

& bequeath the records of my illness
to some thankless think tank.

MINOR FLOOD

No more thunder: the flood recedes
we'll have to comb our hair & get dressed

lose all sense of place—stop being stupid
depressed, pretending to be poor

old, cracked, living on village edge
down by railroad tracks in wetlands

after Equinox in some unnatural dusk
of graveyards & Queen Anne's Lace

no more lost-in-the-19th-century fantasies
traffic flows again—all murk is dispersed

the dangerous angel of rain recedes
over mountains w/ a burden of cloud.

Poems

Somewhere you're blackmailing me
but I never got the note.
We know we know
night covers day
Winter is our shaykh
but still we never dare.

TECHNONECRONOMICON

Under the rose
hides another rose.
Always approached
never broached.
The sign seemed to say
Institute for Human Unfoldment
like origami in Flatland
w/ eldritch trapezoidal angles.
Product code in the
shadowless glare.
You might well seek to
embrace muffled shadows
midnight suns, horrid mysteries.
Proud of their bodies w/out organs
triumph of the New Eugenics.

SWAMP ANGEL

language itself was the first
action at a distance
blue jewel bruises, white bites
abracadabra'd out of plosives & labials
elf-shot thunderstorms.

Call & response
moistured air carries the
weight of words
          & we take responsibility
for all the "lost years" & "lost dauphins"
& the brilliant artificiality of
          Sanskrit or Latin.

Then writing must be doubly so
if only there weren't so much of it, reeds
bending in the wetlands of my heart
you win, admit it, this
                    war of words.

AMBER

1. Bernstein

half jigger Vavilov's Tincture of Hemp
one jigger absinthe, sugar, ice-water, shake
static electricity buzzing, hair stands on end
suddenly Nazis invade the Room
Count zu Solms-Laubach the SS art historian
packs the walls in crates, ships them to Prussia
stashed in "lost subterranean ice room or
mineshaft in the Ohdruf" and never recovered
died with lips sealed. So there we were
floating disembodied over Baltic beach
Clothed With The Sun, that sort of thing,
heads swelled up disappeared & left us
translucent resinous Tears of the Heliades
in a time-warp syrup of vanished Room.

2. Bug Porn

color of a cup of tea
once served to Kublai Khan
slow, packed w/ Time
a pair of beetles caught
in flagrante delicto
down to the DNA
eternal love
in the palm of yr hand
the hand of Kublai Khan still
holding that tea
with his long sharp fingernails
sheathed in gold.

3. Tulipomania

calligrams licked on marbled paper
ink compounded of amber & musk
& meerschaum, petrified urine
& sperm of mermen, culture as
shared hallucination, resins, waxes,
aromatic gums & exudates, coagulation
of sadness detached from any brain
lacquers, electuaries, honeys, loukoums & tars
tears shed in the
Age of Dinosaurs.

4. Vagabondage

Lucky so much of the Past survives.
Slow Glass. Conservatism of amber
delays, retards, O Wandervogel O
Eidelweiss Pirates O nude sunworshippers
of the German Left—think
what Science could've achieved by now
if not for the emergence of the State.
Spirits are attracted to such odors
flies or lizards stuck in our thoughts.

5. L'envoi

Tiger melts into pile of pancakes
butter & syrup, rich puddle
glinting in the sun
the mind if nothing else
free to think
another day.

(for Dale Pendell [r.i.p.]. Liaizon Wakest,
  Wm Strangmeyer)

REBUS

Virginia creepers begin to
glow w/ their own self-light
shoals of tiny phosphorescent shrimp
in the Indian Ocean, the whole point
of paganism being that worship of one
invariably involves you in another &
another: Flypaper of the Gods
tar-babies, in-laws, persons Who
Came to Dinner & Stayed, flies
buzzing in greasy smoke.

Hermes the Third, guest, parasite, thief
bird-headed baboon, green man
bastard of the Moon. Then
they begin exchanging masks
crossdressing & adultery. Sin divinizes.
By definition they do what Thou Shalt Not
leering in at every window: incest, sodomy
impure food, poisons, kidnappings
raptures, continual drunkenness

for instance a pond & willow scene
thru a Moon Window, face by Arcimboldo
rebus, peering faun—and that's
the magic of dirty windows (as
Freddy the Pig used to say) windows
etched with frost like acid glass
in a 19th century Dublin pub

Landscape as Face: The Care &
Cultivation of Cobwebs. Every day is
Halloween. Too much Boehme, Wm Law,
Swedenborg's Dreams, the Choice of Emblems
James Clarence Mangan, Melmoth, The Monk
Novalis & Hoffmann—one god
melts into another then another
more rain smears the windows
erases the house.

Runaways plan on islands where they'll stay
& break the rules. Fox & Crow know the road
you won't turn into donkeys, that's
school propaganda. You need a sugar rush.

Artificial floating island five square miles
never found twice in the same latitude
or longitude—floating Phalanstery where
Harmony is attained thru Mutual Passions

& not the black turnips & stale macaroni
of the therapeutic State. Every house
a tree house or flimsy palace—combination
gypsy camp & Wildwood New Jersey

fairy lights & far-away music always
disappearing over various cerulean horizons.

(For Carolee Schneemann)

Cling to Winter, don't let Winter go
from gelid woods where time is running slow
discolored porcelain shards of rotten ice
the archaeological remnants of the snow

I dream I'm one of a gang of selfish giants
hoarding up all narratives like nuts & port
what Prince of Spring could resent this frozen garden
boarded up like some bankrupt Nordic resort?

Perhaps we should spend our Summers in Patagonia
Antarctic whalers lost in the Seventh Clime
in insulated igloos musty with sleep
away from the migraine pulse of vacated time

exiled till Autumn, wanderers & rovers—
and not come back till Club Med freezes over.

25% of black swans are homosexual
"the unnatural is also the natural"
dark matter is involved or
implicated in the very air we breathe

we could be living in melancholy ruins
of a decayed culture, slouching around
Ottoman rubbish or the potshards of
1907 under the suffocating weight

of all that dark energy—which
has the sinister perverse beauty
of black swans creaking overhead

over some sword-&-sorcery landscape
heavy with remorse over some
black lake or ebony grove.

The alphabet are fish
& assuage no one's dirty regrets
over sins of omission—a narrow voice
that jibbers & squeaks in souterrains
tunnels & vaults—uncanny maybe
but hardly apocalyptic. Fish
in veritable hecatombs fillet'd
& laid down in deepest cellars
of the Ziggurat at Eridu first of many
& oldest of the Eld—the fish
of civilization itself. Bury enough
stinking fish & finally after millennia
you get the alphabet—dry fruit
of a dead sea—corpses of thought.

FIBONACCI'S AIRSTREAM

Fibonacci's curve describes the snail
stop me if you've heard this before
or any involute whose spiral
delineates the exo-esoteric axis
& resultant topology of a hermit crab
hypersensitive introverted our St Anthony
Abbot's convoluted sluggish monk's hood
from beneath which three lurid eyes
like embers palpate the sensorium, our
chitinous nebular Baudelairean slimeball
Van Gogh's ear or motile nipple of a
baroque frog madonna via
slo-mo dervish rotation: romantic
ruin with an extreme dimension turned
in on itself & tucked (as real
estate developers like to say)
away from modernity's stresses.

ILLEGALISM: THE POETRY
OF TOMORROW

We'd run it off in small batches like moonshine
seven times distilled in glass alembic flask
its coil running thru cold mountain rivulet
gathered like dew on felt blankets dragged
at dawn across ragged meadows: potent poteen
its illegality a sign of grace.
There are bars in Harlem & shebeens
in Donegal where customers happily pay more
for 'shine than anything w/ the government chop
a) because it's probably cleaner and
b) because a little crime is itself psychotropic.

GNOSTALGIA

If only we hadn't been kept apart
by malignant conspiracy, a verdigris
of vanished slanted light
of gnoseological nostalgomania
not for the past but the passed
seen from the melancholy perspective
of inorganic unintelligible speed.
Anything faster than a fast horse
is faster than light—especially
this October glimmer so translucent
but so heavy.

BED AS A TYPE OF HEAVEN

Oblomovism
Somnocracy
Little Nemo
Claustrophilia
the old odorous dog
closes the curtains of the
tent of sleep

TABLET

A day without humans
is a day gained
—here in the future
where you're lurking
as a hurricane named
for a saint. Fate
is statistically
inevitable as groceries
especially the dreamiest
& most addictive—
as if a green ray singled
you out from the vulgar crowd.

Bats have achieved the mammalian dream
fast but inaccurate—ladies fear for coiffures
in China symbolize happiness—why not?
souls long to soar. Snakes copulate by the
dozen in the grass—don't disturb them or
you'll turn into a girl. Two snakes on a stick
equals language, the secret hinge of the year.
Children impersonate the uneasy dead and
forgive us in exchange for sugar & silver.

Past erupts into Present like hot lava
blurting from underground volcano vents
Yellowstone gyser from pharaonic caverns
where it wintered over, hibernated bearishly
in a dim dream of itself, bloodless & wan.
10,000 top opera hats spurt into the sky
silky ravens with diamonds in their beaks
BLAM the whole Library of Alexandria
rains papyrus like confetti at an astronaut's parade.
A crack opens in the sidewalk & pedestrians
hurtle through down into 1934, 1911, 1881
crawl out bruised dazed weeping w/ emotion.
Next day all the cracks are sealed
mass amnesia—the anomaly erased
reports suppressed & only a few remember
but say nothing. But even so
one has to admit that lingering post-
eruption dust makes for spectacular
sunsets over New Jersey, Land of the Dead.

a temporary secession
a crime against property
Space has been mapped but time
may still contain anomalies
explosions of nebulosity & idleness
tender land-mines
dumped in reservoirs
like LSD

The pleasure of wandering is equalled only by
the luxury of having nowhere to go.

MIMEO

1.
darned blithe, this sunshine

2.
find an old "spirit duplicator"
& resuscitate it; in the dream
we called it rhodography

3.
Isn't there something authoritarian
about "good weather"?

4.
and something esoteric about "bad" weather?
No one seeds clouds w/ bi-planes anymore.
Watch the bees refuse to shop.

5.
Roseate portals.

THE LATE NEOLITHIC COOKBOOK

Cuisine of secret societies devoted to chthonic
fermentation: yeast: transmutation: grass into milk
milk into butter, flowers into honey—triple stomach
to which we add this china tea. Inside the house it's
still 1795: a light diet, i.e., a diet rich in light.
A perfect day for being Irish. Calving & churning & kneading
gnostic morsels, archaic dumplings in the unprocessed
stew of the continuum. Prince Kropotkin appears at the
kitchen window: is that his beard seen from behind the glass
or the reflection of clouds upon its surface? Imagine him
naked & setting fire to his own house in the shape of a
giant fraise-de-bois: one bite contains the whole of Summer.

RAPTURE

Trees & shrubs begin to uproot themselves
float slowly into the air then gaining speed
vanish over the horizon. Blade by blade
grass follows in upwards rain
& all the most distinctive rocks & stones
arise like big swamp bubbles—gone.
Nothing remains but housing developments
named after the missing features
Shrub Acres, Rockview Park, etc.
& altho we cling desperately
to the last escaping maples
& helium-light crags as they
lift off we have to let loose lest they
take us with them into nothing.

POGO

Eutopia:
the only source of electricity
                              is eels
Herons at sunset return beneath
hangings of spanish moss
                              Swamps
represent the Will To Power As
Disappearance.
                   Forgetfulness of death
is a kind of sideways immortality.

The first australopithecine to use language
was already aestheticizing politics. So what?
The next messiah will be a tree hugger
with a gun—save the whales or I'll kill you.

Everyone from Krazy Kat to my
Uncle Melvin has thought of raising
watermelons on moonshine but sadly
it doesn't work. Where are the sadhus
sitting out the season of steam in
shady cemetaries stoned to the gills?
Fruit becomes mandatory.
Instead of mangoes we used to have
peaches as good as oral sex.
And you know what
          happened to *them*.

CONCEPTUAL INSTALLATION

Dear Sâr Péladan, here's my proposal for
historical reenactment of yr Rosicrucian Mass
w/ music by Erik Satie. First we need
a virtuoso to record score on mechanical player piano
(circa 1907) to simulate ghost of Satie (invisible).
In candlelit chamber decorated as per rubrics
celebrants will be lifesize mechanical automatons
(not electrical) presided over by clockwork Sâr Péladan
in full vestments & Assyrian beard. Spoken parts
pre-recorded & played on wax cylinders
(Edison originals w/ large horns shaped
like black trumpet flowers)—all the machinery
openly displayed—with Bunraku-style
attendants in black to wind everything up.

HAIKU

"The most euphonious phrase in the
English language is 'barn door.'"
—Mark Twain

He opens the barn door
    sees a river meander
        effervescent soda water.

CANNABILOPOLIS

This small tin box for grass is so old
by now there must've bloomed an
entire civilization of sub-molecular sentient
marijuanites inside it w/ vast cities
Babylonian pueblos cave dwellings of Göreme (Turkey)
by Gaudi or Max Ernst hundreds of storeys tall
windows of various shapes not in rows
but cryptic patterns—miles high
semi-conical towers resembling cyclopean hills
of green sparkling crystalline pure THC
& the grass-mites as I think of them
(who knows what they call themselves?)
green humanoid sylphs of indeterminate gender
w/ skin like the milky underbellies of frogs.

RIDDLE

Blame Mallarmé for the hole in the poem
snipped w/ his delicate scissors in the shape
of a fan or a heart: the missing subject.
Like Charades: your body itself a rebus
a living hieroglyph. (Note: why have no grade-A poets
ever composed in this last genre?)
Reconstruct the whole fucking mastodon
from one mandible. A blank intaglio
white-on-white. Someone's just left the room
in a waft of psychic perfume. The wake
of the boat without the boat.
The brown rectangular stain where the
                              painting used to hang
the aunt who lives in the attic who's
                              never mentioned
the secret everyone knows but is never discussed.

Inside every poet a shoe salesman
struggles to get out—each poem
a shoe. This book is our little boutique
where we kowtow before you like
Malagasy slaves begging you
to step on our necks. Each page
gives off a waft of cordovan & suede
mingled with stale socks & the
salesmen's brillantine. Crinkly paper
lines the fetishy boxes like lotus petals.
Back in the 1950s we had an
X-ray machine to reveal yr gracile
green metatarsals & phalanges
your perfect transversal arch.

ARITHMOSOPHY

Certain numbers can make hearts race
blood pound eyes blue near swoon
not as nouns but adjectives modifying
things the chaste Hypatia never
smelt amongst the platonic salads
& pythagorean beans—numbers to make the
tailor tremble till fragile chalk snaps
between nerveless fingers—numbers to
be-sweat the shoe salesman abject
on his gabardine knees—stats
that force statisticians to cross their legs
& groan like elephants in musth—
numbers drifting away from their signifiers &
hovering above our beds like holograms.

BOG ART

Cut crop circle ditches in bogs &
allow them to erode

special tools for cutting peat with
layers of lard

clods of peat to build castles &
set them on fire

build crannog in bog & live in it

Bog Butter

counterfeit hoards of gold torcs
counterfeit bog mummies made of wax

Festival of the Bogs

Nothing but bog for miles around. Rain.

BOG is Slavic for God.

HYPNEROTOMACHIA

Strife of Love in a Dream—and
even there you play hard to get,
evasive. For decades I wandered
thru golden timeworn renaissance perspectives
of a walled city where somewhere I've
lost yr address. Back then
still ignorant of Italy that light was pure
foretelling that color that Tuscan
garden wall in a certain slant of sun
that Mandelstam defined as "Civilization"—
but with de Chirico-esque aspects
such as child's shadow running
after shadow of a hoop in
long late afternoon silhouette.

Joe Miller (1684-1738) The Joke Book
compiled post-mort by someone named Motley
minor Drury Lane actor & wit he was
reincarnation of Priapus the garden-guardian
funny ha-ha and funny-peculiar, carved from
the greensward. Our plaster gnome his
eunuchoid grand-nephew leers as we
filter out of Sunday School. Lurking flasher
vulgar joker talking penis he wards off
the Evil Eye, America being par excellence
the land of envious blight. Flowers should
be forced to wear pants because
they're sex organs. Nature guffaws
as it sodomizes yr Protestant conceits.

LOCUSTS

or cricket Minimalists stretch their glass sheet
the Pandit would've loved that one-note raga
that severe pre-mammalian anaesthetic
disspacement in Time: Einstein w/ a
frontal lobotomy: one brilliant "equals"
"equals" "equals" all summer long glissando
sonic glissade, a single consonant from outer space.
Nobody's riled. Nobody's young.
Embalmed in an opium of false teeth
& castanets you travel for light-aeons only
to get back before you left. One thought
takes seventeen years. Same thought
is best thought—the acoustics of
evolutionary success, the soundbox of sex.

"There are some things Man was not meant to know"
as the Doctor always says in the third reel
so chauvinistically but accurately. We
could've been antiquarians, learned Tocharian
or Sumerian or Indo-European with all its
little stars. The Liberation Front for
Dirty Old Men expresses a poignant
nostalgia for long-lost ideologies
of impossible tenderness. Snow or no snow
sooner or later we'll have to hike out
to the all-nite Mobil station for butter & eggs
& cigarette papers. Born to sorrow as sparks
fly upward we'll avert our eyes from the headlines.

In order to function at all we must envision
an abstract platonic unsolid vapor
in the shape of a South American Colonial Baroque angel
tricorn hat w/ ostrich plume—18th century
silk & lace—sporting a blunderbuss embezzled w/ gems
ambiguous smile of a fox spirit
hands of a marzipan Madonna
possibly Uriel. Now we're cooking w/ gas
seething by gaslight. A kind of hermetic chaos
like Buster Keaton's automated bed
that dumps him upright into his shoes.
Goaded by angel prod & dosed
with angel tea we manage to face
yet another day of the absence of angels.

NEPENTHE—what a marketing concept
elixir that grants surcease of sorrow
origin of recreational chymistry the search
for some ganymedian nectar
                        not forgetfulness
                                    exactly
but jovian altitude
                        gentle precipitation
from the opiate clouds around Olympus
exudation from the Eleusinian fungus
of temporary immortality
                        DON'T REPENT
        DRINK
                        NEPENTHE ! ! !
& forget the I.O.U. Blues for tonite
in the dreamy green & black marble high
silent halls of Hypnos
                        CHOOSE THE
                        GATE OF IVORY,
                                            fool,
the secret recipe available on every
                        supermarket
                                    magazine
                                            rack
poppy mandrake melatonin
                        pheromones of sleeping beauty
popular oblivion
            revel of anonymous masks.

Atlantis was actually New Jersey
West Cape May—a few ruins still
pocked the beach & just offshore an enormous
experimental concrete-hulled ship half-sunk
suspended forever in a child's coloring-book
of crayon waves—all this was our
sunken City of Lys where bells were heard
from beneath the tides. Diamonds literally
littered the sand. Atlantis—
amusement pier garish giant pinball machine
jukebox stinking of dank brine saltwater taffy
going down for the third time—
eels magnetically forced to return again
forever to the Sargasso of thalassic New Jersey.

A species that invents the picnic can't be
all bad. Wicker basket, metal cups that
fold up like accordions, huge thermoses
lined inside w/ magic mirrors & mummied in tartan
chickenparts rolled in cornmeal & cracked pepper
deep-fried in lard, jug wine, cornbread
a nap in the shade & Fitz Omar himself
could ask nothing more, perhaps a Thou
to get a crush on & go for a walk
together into the woods looking for
Herkimer diamonds or garnets, a swimming hole
to fall naked in under heavy trees
plus a 30-pound watermelon: paradise enow.

A ludicrous speeded-up motion
like Hong Kong Kung Fu movie kicks
has afflicted the res publica with
political Alzheimer's like a gigantic spliff
made of 100 zigzag papers for easier
long-term memory loss or "Black Hole Aphasia"
as we dogmatists say—words like UFOs
slipping over the event horizon on hostage carrier waves
that even the FCC can't deregulate. We have ways
of making you talk, Earthling, anal probes
tissue samples, tunnels under area 51
but who cares? "I've fallen and I can't get up."
Big deal—you could say the same for Byzantium or Cathay:
the robot answers but no one ever returns yr call.

The hole in the middle of the poem
might've been terrorism heresy desire
race money sociopathic rage
                    irrepressible memory
someone else's intellectual property
language itself. Possibly, even probably, it's a
dichtergeist (if that's proper Deutsch) a
spectral ectoplasmic hieroglyphic revenant
from the realm where words are animals
& walk like an Egyptian: mysterious
cold spots, spooks that disappear
when you think you've hit them w/ yr car
at night speeding down tree-lined avenue
a deer a woman in a black dress
a discarded ideology a bird against yr windshield.

What we want is a concrete example of the invisible
a religion with stuff that really works
so cleverly no one ever mentions your name
you have no address cannot be located by GPS
you are, as they say, legend—but not
like some superannuated rock star—more like
John Dillinger or Rasputin. You were
an unwitting agent & to this day remain
unaware of yr role in those events—
the perfect witness. You were
temporarily accessed, let's put it that way
by non-State agents or discarnate entities
but now they've vacated the premises
just as you yourself have abandoned the poem.

Thus Nerval's insistence that we steal back
the secret of hieroglyphs from those evil Freemasons
the ones who hanged him in the alley with the raven
in 1855 for daring to found a rival lodge
                    THE ORIENT PEARL
as is wellknown even now in certain circles in Paree.
Verb sap. Finger to nose. Say no more.
Poetry as quintessential hermetic projection
aims to put a little strange english on the
cue-ball of language and sink the 8.
Bards weep & you could collect their tears.

NOVALIS

1.
Cosmogony starts with Old Night.
Read it in yr own Bible.

2.
dream of an ancient Mesopotamian sect
that traced an entirely different set
of constellations—the "Wolf Star"
(Sirius?)

3.
Sissies love the Moon.
And I am of the Sabians
the Moon worshippers of Harran
hymns to the night
the face of Novalis

4.
Say no more.
Whites Off Earth

5.
a culture of Envy so intense
it emits rays that can sicken infants &
kill fruit trees

6.
Money is dromological, a form of speed
nazi amphetamine

7.
Musoleums of simulacra
what Novalis calls the
poeticization of science

8.
but some facts are shy.
Fortean. Fortuitous.

9.
Restore Lost Nature

10.
Sphinxism.
Guerilla topiary.

11.
contra-dance to the
thanaterotic dirges of our failed messiah
Chladni diagrams reveal the letters
inherent in Nature, astral sonograms

12.
Dionysian socialism. Mass Endarkenment.
Up till dawn in the Palace of Night.

7 bottles of Planetary Elixirs one for each box.
Crumpled packets of Turkish & Egyptian cigarettes.
Toy automobiles transfixed with iron nails.
Blue birds' eggs, blown empty. Dead white moths.
Sepia toned pornographic postcards from Tunisia.
Dried lizards from Chinese pharmacy.
Engravings of mandalas from Agrippa.
Gris-gris from the grave of Marie Laveau
labelled & packed in red cloth sachets.
Cheap pulp copies of Mexican Dreambooks.
Assorted Chinese firecrackers w/ gaudy labels.
Miniature white swans carved in marzipan.
Leave boxes in 7 vacant lots such that plotted on a map
they form the rough shape of a human body.

LINKED AUTISM SONNETS

(For Th. Metzger
         & Jake Rabinowitz)

1.

Suddenly it turns out we're all autistic
"a state of mind characterized by daydreaming
hallucination & disregard of external reality"
Suddenly across the desk the therapist
(alert vibrant keen rational) stares
at the big-eyed sad child end of the spectrum.
You. Us. The mind in the cave. Lascaux. The flickering light.
Does he await some Darwinian Singularity
to emerge as eerie blond cold children
from outer space w/ strange powers
or are they detritus left behind
by Money's evolutionary quantum leap to
the cool clear triumph of the light?
Either way it's a win/win situation.

2.

The Slow Snow Movement. Snow is autistic
the way it closes you in & induces reveries
out of touch with external reality
to the point where the very phrase
external reality begins to shimmer and
stink like dead mackerel in the moonlight.
Sleepy snow lacks affect & its trick of never
repeating itself exactly once in infinity makes it an
idiot savant, morose wizard of autistic artistic wastes.
Nietzsche on thorazine. Lost inside that cloud
of unknowing or refusal to know like eskimos in
igloos—houses of snow that seem to glow
in a universe of snow you discover the obsessive repetition
of heraldic beasts heals the wounds of time with scabs of imagery.

3.
Next thing you know it's Arctic Hysteria & the
breakdown of all barriers between Show & Tell.
The self is like the Port Authority Bus Terminal—
eventually you get through it. Only the crystal tears
of gifts or glyphs mark the way out of this labyrinth of mistletoe
& sacrificial exchange. What cave paintings mean
is unimportant. What's important is that they mean.
Charm School Chain Gang. Bow to the god of snow
for permission to enter this temporary autistic zone.
Market democracy waters down the thunder & sells it back
for obscene profits. "Autistic Awareness" indeed.
What appears from a distance a kind of fairy changeling
seen close up is the mirror of the self
in the eldritch glow of missing emotion.

ADVERTIZING BROCHURE FOR
MAIL-ORDER HOODOO SCHOOL OF
HIEROGLYPHICS &
PROTECTION FROM THE EVIL EYE

"The School is the Finger,
 the Post Office is the Moon."

Hermes is himself the critique of communication theory
hieroglyphic parsing of the textolatry he
patronizes. Eleggua, santo of thresholds who
must be given rum & cigars or else he
scrambles the eggs of noise. Purple assed baboon.
Change money meester? One thin dime
the erectile element in yr thermometer
yr Rough Guide to the World of the Dead
half hermaphrodite half heron, your
Hudsonian Hermes, he's the "herm" in "hermeneutic"
trouser snake as writing implement
prickpocket vagabond offshore banker
crapshooter & electromagnetic impulse
like those children w/ green hair found in a
Welsh cave, escapees from the Hollow Earth.

Some disenchanted evening
in a rapture of boredom
the lilacs of resignation will
not be moved. Spectral Linnaeus
will pass unrecognized amongst the throng
of sit-com stars his paper lantern
pulsing with glowworms searching for someone
dishonest enough not to be dull.
Formal Linnaeus however is appalled
& pallid enough to be mistaken for
Erasmus Darwin his doppelganger. The scent
of lilac weighs so heavy on this
crepuscular atmosphere that the two of them could
switch genders or even species.

TABLET
FOR TIAMAT

goddess of neolithic Kropotkinite midden heaps
who hates the clangor & bustle of metallurgic Marduk
with his Plan-ism for Planetary Progress
defend us now in this Babylon of light pollution
take back the night for blackness & the
slumber of demons, the superstitious saturnalia of
Endarkenment. If we can't have yr Chaos at least
spread out yr pall of inefficiency & sloth.
Accept our somnolence as homage, we yr fellahin
yr cyberserfs yearning to be shiftless as Neanderthals.
The polyamory of Beardsley's Under the Hill is yr
purest orthodoxy. Your lurid flickering Boschianism
(already censored in the cuneiform version) melts

the banks

(the first temples) like lava in a wetdream. Stymie
the emergence of Weberian Capitalism. We support
the Politics of the Worst, we who read ROMA backwards
deaf to Pavlov's Bell we hope to pay no bills
& salivate only when there's something to smell.

Let's return to Hollow Earth via
the giant decenseur at Mt Erebus
all brass & teak, pneumatique
like a Bell Epoque ballroom
sinking beneath Antarctic schlag
slowly slowly (not to get the bends)
suddenly the Art Nouveau windows
disclose the panorama of rapturous deep
a cavern so high & vast it vanishes
in the distance. Blue waterfalls
fall for miles and break up on
crags in spumes of mist, clouds lit
by vast artificial globes set into
cave walls by unmentionable science.

(for Yvan Goll,
Pope of Surrealism)

A politique of the marvelous demands
conceptual Brocéliandes of Neolithic
weltwald, a Black Forest stretching
from the Altai Mts to Altoona PA
thru which democratic shamans &
selfchosen chivalric elites can collide
with "the bright lightninglike flash
known as triboluminescence" of struck
quartz pebbles or Arthurian knights.
Forget Marinetti's plan to bomb the museums
we propose the Waters of Lethe—balm
of short-term memory loss bottled in
crystal flasks that sparkle spontaneously
in the dusk. Eau de Lotus.

A day lost in lethargy & mooning
over the Fifties—there's no there there
we smirk—you can drive forever & never
arrive. That's why we get this nagging feeling
that if we stop moving we'll sink back
into some temporal shallows where alienation
is still bliss. An overcast October day
drugged w/ too much sleep as refuge
from the very suffocation it induces—
a homeopathic overdose. In the city
I know you're weary but in the country
we're quaint. No unsupervised play.
No burning leaves. Just because innocence
is ignorance is no reason to despise it.

Weather condition as psychic skin
coat or cloak, flesh that by comparison
would be bone & unfeeling. We sense
through weathers that become us (in a
flattering sense) or become us (in an
ontological sense) but without specific content—
like drugs. But since weather is someone or
something else does that make us
parasitic or symbiotic? Earth's skin
our skin—a pathetic fallacy neither
trivial nor untrue—would be too much
to hope for & yet groovy as if
mist over the mountain were approaching
like the portrait of an unknown self.

Winter a giant wigwam or commune-sized
quonset hut woven of reeds & mud
snowbound hortus conclusus of stone soup &
mythopoesis, each atomized consumer alone
each oedipal unit squared off by
inanimate walls from the howling etc.
praying against sex demons & antivivisectionist
terrorists, yearning for vestiges of
an almost forgotten civilization, brooding
on tax avoidance, real estate deals
bourgeois super-egos & seed catalogues.

Truly a can of worms eh
comrades? Pump yourself up
to a 19th-century neurasthenic glee
at other people's gardens
or the love of ruins, vast sycamores
cracking the rubble of abandoned Walmarts
the breathless obituaries of
bats & bees, the relentless pompes funèbres
of lost languages retired to some
gated Isle of Inisfree Home for
Assisted Living. Because only shared illusions
ever come true, like the Man in the Wig
who's his own best customer or the
lingering tone of music dying on the breeze.

ESCAPISM

Swear fealty to the dark leprechaunism of revenge
become a lump of sensual actuality in the thin gruel of
spectacular electromagnetism.
Set your basement afloat.

Behind the iron curtain of sheer boredom
with Civilization as we know it, psychic
discoveries proliferate & angelic sensations
are a dime a dozen
like a dirigible sleepy with nitrous oxide
finally so attenuated it trances us with
streaming sensations of thinking we
remember what it was.

The Escapist Militia practises reenactments
costumed complete with powdered wigs
of great moments in the history of haute cuisine
a fantasia of negation.

Obsessions are veritable Galapagoses of elegant ennui
Renounce the emptiness of vacations for the pleroma of
permanent unemployment, the vaguely impenetrable
                                    isles of the blest.
Even short thunder showers swell the head like a grape
& make it blush. The storm is a coast & briefly
we're degenerate wreckers eager to pilfer
whatever flotsam washes up on our distant shore.

TIME TRAVEL

Those who inhale these alien spores drift back in time &
temporarily indwell the bodies of long gone smokers who in
turn have wafted off to even earlier dates & remoter climes ad
(perhaps) infinitum. In 1911 these devotees of extra-terrestrial
mycoremediation are disguised as opium addicts in Fu
Manchu's Limehouse den beneath the Thames. Off I go for one
gilded soporific transmigratory augenblik & while I'm vacant
who knows what nostalgist from the 23rd century passes thru
my empty brain.

Too bored to sustain the vibratory level of incessant Progress we
slump toward the portholes like so many rats, clamber down the
ropes & scuttle off on a suave-qui-peut basis in search of some
consolatory mania.

Tropicalismo
Orientalismo   } each with its favorite
Nostalgismo   bistro
Horizontalismo

turns in on itself & dissolves into a tableau vivante of
sentimental anniversaries & badly printed newsletters
a college so invisible so diaphanous
so secret some of its members don't even
know they're in it.
A shimmering glow of Düreresque melancholia
suffuses the twilite of Kapital.
So sue me. And go to yr grave with regrets
for the winged words you wasted.

Is. Is. Is. The tyranny of the intransitive.

Aubrey Beardsley in suburban New Jersey
in 1957 thinks he's trapped in the
fat boy like Felix the Cat in a bottle
of india ink—superhero stuck

in his secret identity scared to jump.
But he jumps. Thank god for LSD.
The whole gang has been reincarnated.
Few days are so pleasurable as those
on which one quits a job. Crime pays.
Slowly slowly one makes up for having
died so young last time.

Is it possible to remember a smell
or is the smell itself the memory?
If only our manifesto
could attain the rhetorical felicity of
the Acme Catalogue of Heirloom Roses.
As in the French Assembly
if you're reactionary enough you suddenly
find yourself on the Left, so also
with roses. Talk about yr
poesie trouvée. If only!
An incense that explodes & knocks over the
tapers & shreds the ikebana.

If smells have color this one's tinged with back-to-school acedia like
a vast field of superannuated sunflowers down to a riverbank where
no one is swimming. I'd call it nostalgic but any smell is nostalgic,
wallpaper in a room where you once recovered from some disease.

Unfortunately utopia was all too affordable
a politics that begins at my door & ends only
in floods of tears
our only innovation being to admit defeat &
plan the retreat into some no-go Chernobyl
where we can become the monsters we are.
"Life is elsewhere" but accessible.
Temporary ruins.

We await the withdrawal of Heaven's
Mandate from the fabric of
reality itself, potential possession by

ancient voices prophesying the
usual punch-up. Houdini,
sever the effluvium of yr ectoplasm.
Please evade "maturity", the last
two minutes before death.

Time itself is lunar. It swells. It diminishes. Space is solar.
Electricity doesn't conquer darkness—it erases stars. Night
equals right. Crushed velvet. Pre-industrial musk. Only slaves
could conceive of heaven as unrelieved daylight. Escapism's
paradise lies in the shadows of the Moon.

Sailing to an island
ions ozone iodine delight
dappled light bewilders but
sharpens appetite. Raoul Dufy, meet
Winslow Homer. Pascal would've bet on
Neptune—a brine-drunk existentialist
seduced by German nudism.
All islands are Celtic. One is saintly
one drinks a lot
because so little is actually at stake
in these pro-tem clandestine eutopias.

The Junkyard of History turns out
to be an OK vacation destination
a sort of Guadalajara, low rents, sunshine.
Surely Hermes is patron of garbage
as secret form of writing.
The Dump is our power spot
its mephitic memorial gasses the
source of our philosophic fire.

Up until now Art has revealed secrets
but henceforth its goal will be
to keep them.

The demi-maudit or half-damned poet
hedges his bohemian debts & consoles
self with a few consols at four percent
doling out the laudanum in sensible
teaspoons like crusty port. His inner Jeckyl
embraces his inner Hyde thanx to new
age therapeutics allowing him to project
animus outward & avoid the Chattertonian
telos or Artaud's electroshock. His
convulsions remain mental, he controls his
full-moon urges & sublimates them into
semi-masterpieces.

Anticipation of violets & lilacs
the key to the mysteries is narrativity
the heart of the story a human being
made out of flowers—snowdrops—skunk
or music—anything but these words
each of them two-faced as a coin.
A culture based on inhalation of attars.

Think global
                act yokel
a hayseed hedgerow scholar
w/ Ovid in pocket
                        site specific as
the corpse beneath the hearth
gnomon to yr own shadow
                        Bakuninist
to all would-be conquistadors
of the Moon, the
                    sublunary
waters & airs.

WATERFALL IN
MOOSALAMOO, VERMONT

No amount of scientific know-how or
nil admirari can damp the squib of
our satori, no eco-tourism can
vitiate the baraka. From our
hidden guerilla basecamp
in the feminine hills we launch
our assault on heaven. Why
is the sky blue? Not
how, but why?

OOLONG

Hopped-up sounds like just
the ticket. Even little peak
experiences don't come cheap.
Spend cash like water—in fact
buy water. Surrealist soup.
By any means necessary, as
Malcolm X and Baudelaire put it:
remedy for attention-deficit-disorder
or the endless sexual rain of Dublin.

NEW WAYS TO PUBLISH
YR POEMS
(for Home Planet News)

On the backs of prayer-cards to made-up saints. Disguise as
religious tracts & leave them in church vestibules. Or as tourist
brochures & leave them in museums. Or as Missing Cat/Dog
flyers on telephone poles. Or as hiphop graffiti or obscene
scrawls on walls in unlikely public spaces. Sonnets on peel-
off stickers. Hire bums thru temp agencies to carry enigmatic
sandwich-boards. Is it still possible to send telegrams? Wire
1000 haiku to random addresses. Get junk-mail permit for
pulp mass-mailings in targeted neighborhoods. Personalized
poems delivered by messenger pigeons. Buy ad space in yr local
news-rag & run yr own Poetry Corner. Pyrotechnic poems w/
words outlined in gunpowder on huge wickerwork frames. From
hot-air balloon painted w/ hermetic symbols drop leaflets like
Shelley in Ireland, toss them into clouds printed on thin rice
paper. Using water-soluble ink, paint poems on banners & flags
to be washed away by rain or drowned by tides. Engrave odes
on thin sheets of metal or stones & bury them in public parks.
Remember etch-a-sketch? Sky-writing is not as expensive as you
might think—pungent phrases for summer beaches disguised as
sun-tan ad's. Lightbulb displays on Goodyear blimps.

THE WAY TO WEIGH DOWN

Down with down. Go down Moses.
Get down. The one-dimensional State
don't appreciate no downy things.
Down ye croppies. County Down
we picture as a non-viable ambiguity
between two conditions neither solid nor gas
cloudy nebulous fuzzy, like the
modern Persian word for No which is
the archaic Persian word for Yes
or goosedown on adolescents
neti neti as they say in Advaita
no damn way to run a business
plowing all-too-ephemeral
downy interdimensional snow.

ORNAMENTAL HERMIT

An anchor is bent back—an anchorite is laid back—out of the
chorus—out in the outback—stuck in the sand the Coptic desert
that's mapped all over Ireland's face & then re-mapped like the
Odyssey on Upstate New York, each island a planet with its own
little prince—each Ithaca & Carthage with its own grist mill &
opera house its athenaeum or Chautauqua its phalanstery or
Grange. This hermitage devoted to the austerities of Pachomius
& Johnny/Apple/Baptist in the Boschscape waiting on a
sign, a miraculous blossom or syncretic delirium of Serapis
& Trismegistus—disguised as roadside oratorium in the Irish
Catskills or Schoharie Hills—an ornamental hermit for the tourist
trade, a three-star destination for guaranteed edification—the
wispy white semi-bald shoulder-length hair—thin beard—
skullcap—cranky opinions—self-published tracts souvenir
keychains & organic honey. Professional anchorite. Holy Well
(throw silver coins). Petting Zoo of Prophetic Beasts. Raw Food
Snackbar—locust smoothies—showbread & sprouts—watercress
& manna. Signs: Hermit is IN / Hermit is OUT. Behind the barn
& concrete garden with broken bottles & plastic embedded plaster
saints & visionary castles each with its own moral typed label
under bugstained glass—beyond the fence a scraggly woodlot
littered with old refrigerators & half-burnt tires. Puttering in
his little garden of legal psychotropics beside primitive wattled
hut in shapeless Breughelian hat & hairy djellaba while maybe
five cars an hour cruise by & not one stops. Winters are edgy.
One envies one's 18th century forebears their lordly patrons. A
skein of crows imposes itself behind & above the whole scene in
fading midwinter azure limitlessness—a punctuation of crows.
Frozen solid the creek creaks on nights w/out electricity. Egypt
of the Catskills. Cairo in Greene County—With his cat Gregory.
Embarrassing the petitbourgeois families from New Jersey by
asking them to get down on their knees with him & pray to
Nature's God.

SECRECY CREATES VALUE

Rough secrecy means escape from media

Refusal of the Image—the photograph not taken—film left undeveloped—absence-of-image as artform

The poem unwritten—talked away in some pub or café

or if written never published but only read aloud or passed from hand to hand in flawed versions scribbled on backs of envelopes

art that cannot be distinguished from natural magic or the accidental beauty of weather & decay. Buried art. Burnt art. Unrecorded situations

secret art conspiracies. That which does not appear in media scarcely exists—a vast potential Outside

Radio Silence. Poetry as whole-body communication. No need for an underground—just under the radar.

In a story I invent someone
who proclaims Electricity is Sin—
Turn the clock back to the Neolithic
kill the lawyers, let the Spirits in.

The reader smiles—no one calls the cops
this is just literature—anything goes—
these shadows act out our illusions
but nothing counts—as every reader knows.

The author's simply playing w/ these notions
trying on masks, now murderer, now saint
letting other voices speak his secrets
& recite his explanations & complaints.

Mere fiction need no longer fear the State
that deems its crimes too little—and too late.

ENDS

*(For D. Mandl & the Brooklyn
Psychogeographic Society)*

Do the Ends
justify these mean
streets—dead as it were
by definition
w/out modifying adjectives? or
could there be a living
End one might ask?
a cul de sac
of Sartrean psychogeography
still throbbing w/ something
other than signage?
Somewhere a Finesterre
a World's End with a
decent pub?—
old wardrobe or phone kiosk
w/ a hidden dimensional
door to elsewhere? to the Egress?
or is melancholia
itself an elsewhere
an end in itself?

I missed my calling—meteorologist—wasted my life unable to distinguish cirrus from cumulus & never the Nostradamus of any farmer's almanac. I would've militated against the manichaeism of TV weather prophecy & preached zennishly there's no such thing as bad weather, only bad luck. I'd cultivate a cult of inclemency advocating nude rain bathing, sex in snow, a Report for afficianados of February, Full Moon lunacy statistics, zodiacal harvest dates for psychotropic plants, comparative folklore of weather magic. Enter amorous embrace with Earth's felt or pelt of atmosphere via our predictions of falling stars & spells for bells that cause thunder.

JOHN HUMPHREY NOYES GOES INTO EXILE

Train stuck for hours in blizzard
snack-car runs out of hot dogs
drifting toward Niagara
dreams he's locked in a barrel
Flight into Canada
Hiawathan mists

The passenger's eye like a
burglar's glim probes those
old frame houses, rears turned
to the tracks, peers
into back bedroom windows, leers
w/ phantom whistles of longing for
some poorer reality.

Thoth to Aesculapius: over & out
—a drowsy recuperation
eating canned peaches & re-reading
Pseudo-Eratosthenes, he travels
with his favorite diseases
his temporary shrouds
(provided one is taking
                the proper medication
                                of course)
soft as a window on
a nocturnal Nile

a midden heap designed by
                Cagliostro
(can we call it science if it
                never works?)
Recovery from sickness is an ideology.
                        ALL ABOARD!

All canals are a bit Chinese
de Chirico & Piranesi designed canals
contra naturam pulled by mules
thru poppy & tulip fields, the
canal-boat's spatial poetics stretch
attenuated nocturnal spectral
gemutlich by aquaduct passing
by water over water. And the gin
is a-gettin' low. And also
Dutch, miniature blue-&-white world
on a tile, vignette of chinoiserie on
teapot, blue willows along
placid canal with scarcely a
drink till we get to Buffalo.

(for Rudy Rucker)

Collecting some selves from nearby
alternate dimensions I send out
squads of tiny replicants. How
can we bear to be less beautiful
than trees when we might be more-so
they squeak. Can we save myself
by jumping into our own pocket
ad infinitum or will
eventually all such schemes
                          like chain letters
break down & leave the body
holding the bag? The trees nod.
They agree to anything & everything.
No dialectic edge.

A rivulet that creeps
along the backsides of dead farms
& former factories & that lacks
all economic function except as cloaca
for treated waste begins to take on
sinister airs, brown & sad
as if it flowed from the 19th century—
always going away—slightly fecal
like regret—like unwritten history.
Why do I think I spent someone
else's childhood by its banks? because
children live in the 19th century &
still experience their earliest nameless
dreads beside rivers of former times?

LETTER TO MRS LUDD
THE BLACK LAMP

*"...not to suggest a Luddite approach
at this late date..."*
—S. Edwards
The Arts Paper
(Boulder CO, June '01)

"The Revolution will be digitized!"
—C. Clark. ibid

1.

Volunteer to serve the Negation
Never too late for Mrs Ludd
If Bugs Bunny's a Surrealist
what's that make Elmer Fudd?
Wherever you are tonight Mrs L
Tiamat Tara rivernymph undine
Captain Moonlight & Saint Monday
flaneurs on ancient boulevards of spleen
never complain never explain
our secret society goes back to the Neolithic
peonies penises skinsoft rain
the garden—the bicycle—please be more specific.

2.

Perfect Mirror of Global Capital
the Devil's waiting room
haunted slum & universal slime
of TechGnosis & cybergloom
pumpkinification
carpal brain syndrome
public suicide machine
Mammon's dictaphone

Moloch's infernal combustion
psychic noise pollution
landscape of corpselight
metaphoric cold fusion

3.
Very well no longer resist prophetic voices
angry illiterate letter pinned to social factory's door
Neither Physics Nor Metaphysics—empirical morality
haunted by spirits real as need be but poor.
Suburban Luddite. Jungle marches on the city
tear down digital enclosures smash the looms
turn off the hell drone kill the power
light the lying city only with Moon.

4.
Reactionary nostalgist
crackpot Kropotkinite
last human lab-rat gone rabid
ungrateful dynamite

monasteries of slowness
even light goes less than MC^2
cultivate holy datalessness
secrets meant to be shared

How many Lady Ludds
how many General Neds
it was raining when you left us
we forgot what you said

5.
Switch off the Aufklarung before leaving
socialism minus electricity please
Black Light of the alchemists of Isfahan

where even day falls into reveries
Power failure: rain comes in lacquered screens
the house feels like a pelican of glass
phone goes dead but someone else's voice
starts to life like pistils licked by bees
Storm's over: power returns—but not to you
tree-hating landscape-rapists throw the switch
electrocuting all your monastic pleasures
icebox grumbles lightbulbs galvanize
radio threatens more cancerous weather
eliminating all your buried treasures

6.
We lose a world every 15 minutes
by evening nostalgia for morning overtakes us
digital hemlock numbs our limbs to slumber
fearing nothing nice will come to wake us
This IS the Future: how do you like it so far
anachronistic fireflies? Petroleum: a prophecy
(by the author of *Der Golem*) suffocation
600 channels: tombstones: burning seas
Black Lamp dark phosphorescent pearl of night
how many dodo species whacked like weeds
or children vanished into ambient screens
No King but King Ludd asleep beneath the hill
under the parking lot the beach—but who
could be foolish enough to want to smash machines?

7.
note
last known sledgehammer of Luddites
manufactured by Enoch & Co
I see it under glass in the museum
one night begin to glow

[An earlier version—dedicated to Diane diPrima—appeared in *Fifth Estate*.]

ET IN ARCADIA

*(for Bishop M. Aelred Sullivan
 & Fr Michael Bacon)*

*"The human desire for transcendence is
an arguably hard-wired behavior"*
                    —Arcadia Research Project
                    (Australian Network for Art & Technology)

1.

Gnostic Police: mind over matter
what else is law but bad magic?
A fictitious person has no liabilities
                              only assets
no corpse to weigh down its
                              immortal spirit
Sphinx
          vast & vague as a cloud of radioactivity
succubus
               flea that swells to the size of a galaxy
strawberries crossed with the genes of fat people:
El Estupido the unconscious thinks it's all SciFi

2.

High Moral Ground? Y'can't get there from here.
Queer jouissance: class traitor (see Genet)
voluptuous dégringolade—Imaginal Past
down the hole with the trolls: gone away
                    Exiles of Cyberia unite, you've
                    nothing to lose but chains of "Lite"

3.

The old Ukrainian carp fishers
are picking up & moving
slowly out of this Dutch genre canvas—
June & dappled—even the name is Dutch
the Something-Kill
                              From the other bank
you can see they scored at least
                                        one big one
dull gold held up in the ray between
                                                  blue clouds
steamed with dill & potatoes

4.

renunciation laves the skin like rain
silky, spagyric, excised from time but not
from space   BLAMM   thunder defines place
a game of bowls in a valley time forgot
Not that you have anything against time
as continuum rather than torture machine
or the Taylorism of everyday life sliced
& diced & lost to some Maxwellian fiend
In fact the Order proposes a Reconquista
seizing back the provinces of rain
invisible worlds hover behind its screens
Every gadget that disappears makes way
for unpolluted space/time to reclaim
the marches between the banal & the unseen.

5.

Anabaptists on dope: strict observance
Amish icebox spermaceti lamps
under the radar off the grid—in fact
no phone no television & no maps
Entheogenic sacramental heaven
whiling away the time till Armageddon

6.

haven't tied off the veins of pleasure but
just can't stand the tragedy of representation

dunno much theology biology but
shade is as good as a hat

La Physiologie du goût delivers the goods but
the Slow Food Movement's an Escargo Cult

7.

E.T.A. Hoffmann Fan Club
Pro-Endarkenment Left
meet at the bend in the river
between warp & weft

Children on summer lawns
birds at their dawning jamming
nightingales sullen thunder
hunting & farming

Fishing in the manuscriptorium
the stylite in an armchair
stuck in the crook of a willow
prays to empty air

in mourning for all beautiful fleeting thoughts
dispersed by the police. Politics is a scab you can't
help picking. In widower's weeds & crepe
with mutes & black percherons to
haul the catafalque to the crematorium
of Progress. A sob fest. A keen of
theoretical banshees ululating in French.
Each text the epitaph of some defunct
aesthetic shock or spasm of amour fou
rebukes the chorus (brekkakoax) of vain regrets
waters the weeping willows & noir cypresses
of a moribund cryptotheology with
envy & spite. Every word spilled is
another lost baby another hungry ghost.

OTHER PEOPLES' GARDENS

Art-for-art's sake self-indulgence
surrounds Spring with implifications of being
insufficiently depressed or stressed.
Finicky recherché aesthetics of
lilac violets dogwood feral orchards
undisciplined by market forces, smarmy Wordsworthian
faux-zen dandyism of ordinary poor
roadside Proustian day lilies
& bogs of purple loosestrife—gardens
for slackers fin-de-siècle dilettantes
parasites of Nature's most disheveled hair-do—
Spring's flaneurs ignore today's vital issues
lawns gone to seed comfrey chicory raspberry
not flamboyant decay but just
unkempt enough to pass unnoticed.
Even the gardener punches no clock
& must collaborate with worms, too poor
or too stupid for Today's Busy Lifestyle.

THE JUKES

Finally the primal 'scape emerges forlorn shrouded
in tangled bushy bogs & rotten snow
to mingle with hidden Indians, freed slaves
Irish drop-outs & other social scum: homeland
of the Jukes victims of the Eugenic Gaze, degenerate
tri-racial incestuous surly 6-toed
unchurched unschooled unfit sub-hillbillies &
hereditary work-shirkers. Tainted blood
was to blame for their poverty & petty criminality
science concurred because science always agrees
with Power & Money. Eugenics is out of fashion
because of a certain German overenthusiasm
so now we have Human Genomics instead
plus ça change plus la meme chose, eh comrade?

PLUTARCH SWAMP

Nothing resists Progress like a good swamp
Protect Our Wetlands they demand but never
Save the Swamp, the bad part of the subconscious
swarming with creatures we've smothered over with our
bland intentions, tannic broth & seething mire
damped down & shunned by busy daylight
& its smarmy minions. There are no
guided tours of Plutarch Swamp.
Dismal only to the uninitiated
O if only I could live there
how my bourgeois veneer would crumble
my reputation decay. Blue herons
would glide like calligrams across
blue dusks sad & hallucinogenic
chinoiserie, blue white & dun
as an old teapot contemplated daily
from the sagging porch of my
doublewide where the Swartekill fans out
in fens & meres reedbeds & tangles
of blackberry & wild rose north of the
old town cemetery & just west of Pang Yang.
Swamps are the nurseries of cults
Seven Finger High Glister Starry Wisdom Sect
Swedenborgian sex maniac millennialist
crackpots fleeing the everpopular
wrath to come. The Lady in Gray, ghost
of Jemima Wilkinson the Publick & Universal Friend
or rather her telepathic emanation
once worshipped by degenerate schismatics
still seen floating amidst the cracked
nameless gravestones of Pang Yang
while over at the Hunt Club

a cabal with roots in the Paleolithic
shapeshifters, white trash avatars of atavistic
Algonkian animism
possessed by entities more shadowy & antediluvian
than six-pack Saturday nights of lycanthropy
unhinged on moonflowers & black hellebore
practising omophagic rites &
initiatic venery. So flee
into the Swamp
October Country
queer space
realm of Maroons, refuge of
Hessian deserters
conceptual witchcraft
runic landscape of misfit
misanthropes, poling a flatboat
thru cattails we'll spy the
thin blue smoke of a
woodstove like a spirit road
above the hide-out of that
garrulous hermit, our
other self.

SWIMMING HOLE

Dolmens & menhirs mark our flaccid rapids.
No hero salmon no athlete trout
but any fat carp could breast its way up
stream with a few sullen flaps.
Chuang Tzu meets Capability Brown.
A canoeful of Indians only just
slid round the bend. One
has the impression of being an
impressionist. Two
or three might attain
bargain-basement Barbazonian (plein-air)
picnic mit plonk & take-out. Feng shui
draws the languid gaze to an island
too far away to wade to.
Glacial erratics arrange
themselves like placid scholars' stones
thrones for stoners, soaking
up rays dazed as catfish
amidst the venerable trash
of former freshets, mysterious
pieces of New Jersey all parts now
of the same composition.

ANOTHER SWIMMING HOLE

(For Mick Taussig)

Down here with a dehumidifier you
can pump 30 gallons an hour
out of the atmosphere. Freshwater eels
& saltwater eels are the same eels
from the same Sargasso Sea & appear
for obscure Freudian reasons seasonally
rootless cosmopolitans mingling uneasily
w/ the Rondout's honest trout
in fennel & cream sauce. Understanding
the continual emergence of the State
as magic has scarcely augmented
our happiness. Whereas here
the choral gurgles & chortles
of Lorelais & bull frogs
have drowned our tears.

RONDOUT CREEK

High up in mountains creeks have no history, laughing &
crying like babies almost not yet named—then pregnant with
streamlets they gather families, berrypickers, double-wides,
anecdotes—Pompey's Cave where Kripplebush Creek spirts from
sheer rock-face as if dowsed by Moses, or Mombaccus where
the Algonkan Bear God's face carved in sycamore somehow
reminded the Dutch of Bacchus: two creeks rush together in
divine drunkenness. But eventually rivers acquire history, &
History mostly consists of stories about rivers. A canal runs
through the Nineteenth Century: tanneries, pulp mills, cement
mines: river as romantic sewer. But then America stops making
things, history itself corrodes. In the woods you stumble upon
lost cyclopean monoliths—50 years transforms it all back into
legend, blue herons return, signs of economic disaster, spooky
charm of industrial decay, history as a kind of pollution. Slyly
the creek restores its own wildness. All narratives collect & spew
into one big River That Flows Both Ways along with the last few
rusty tugboats & corroded barges. Both ways: in other words
it comes back to haunt us with bats & lightning bugs & a pink
Moon somehow much much more archaic than the concept of
private property.

SWIMMING HOLE: BROKEN AQUEDUCT, MOHONK

Swimming hole as proletarian version of
holy well, eye of the world, your saint
is fey.
        Play, don't pray here
on pain of offending la duende
of 19th century decay.
                I'm saving
this one for a rainless day
in a dry month in the late
post-modern era. Just
visualizing it refrigerates
                the pineal
in a very non-
        Cartesian way.

PLATTEKILL GORGE: WATERMEADOW VIEWED FROM RR BRIDGE

Where are the 19th century Dutch cows
gone with their stinking halos of flies?
Too neolithic too realistic too hindoostani
they've fucked off to BOVINA out in Delaware County
cows of yesteryear
                      with a moo-moo here
mere memory there.
                      Wither too
Farmer Gray, his celtic geese, his
                        triple-X jug
farmer as hipster-clown, his zoological jazz?
Ah, *quelles larmes*. Farmer as spazz
joke-butt of America's sad collapse
went bankrupt sold the stead
fled to Florida & is now dead.
What is a bard? a bard is one
whose life is worth so-&-so many cows
a cowboy poet whose lampoons can cause
skin rash or even death, who eats
the secondbest slice of rosbif
& drinks the king's imported port
vox populi hence quasi-divine.

This creek is named by Carlton Mabee in his
Listen to the Whistle. During the Depression
at a camp called Hobo Rock a farmboy named Earl
recalls his fascination with the hoboes, knew
his parents would disapprove, visited them
anyway when out fishing for pickerel in
Sawmill Brook. They cooked in tin cans, drank
water from the stream, as Earl did too.
Now heaven knows we're depressed again
but we're not farmboys & can't run
away & anyway the railway's been
replaced by a "linear park". No more
hobo jungle, no brass plaque to mark
its vanished site—but still the
same creek, the same melancholy October dusk, the
month for aimless wandering.

JOHN BURROUGHS NATURE PRESERVE

You've been traitor to race
class nation & gender—but
the thrill is gone in the
flatulent aftermath of
Deconstructionism
everything you've lost
or can't afford. The Sage
made a good thing out of
Nature & built this rude hut
to escape his wife
now a museum. So now you
can contemplate what it'd
be like to contemplate
the not-yet-reified &
soon-to-disappear. You can
peer thru the windows & envy
the unimaginable luxury of life
w/out plumbing & electricity.
Same skunk cabbages for
10,000 years—same deer
same starry void
blissfully unaware of how
it's been drained of its
uselessness & declared a
national treasure. Today only!
we offer the notion of
indulging in the most voluptuous
of all treasons, that against
consciousness itself.

POND

(for Levi & Gret)

Liquifact artifact: designer pond
goes Genji. How long before it
outgrows its bulldozer birthmarks
& gets real? Humans
are part of Nature, OK, but
what about aesthetics?

       a recent wound
suppurating à la Fisher King
pond as Grail.

It leaks. Plugged with clay
a gormless face appears
      acne'd in algae
months of silence ensue. Is the pond
some kind of moron? But wait.
One night

a single solitary
lovesick amphibian pilgrim
awakened perhaps after centuries
of mummification in caked humus
or maybe fallen from the clouds
a Fortean egg, a damnable fact—
       one frog
suddenly soliloquizes
& within a few tense nights
    of polluted asterisms

& baking days of suspense in the athanor
of hayseed sun, lo
a responsorium, choral,
                              liturgical
whacked-out sex-crazed &
assymetrical
                    arises

dragonflies arrive like Papal helicopters
word spreads from birds to birds
a new shy nymph has appeared
azure & intelligent, more-or-less
ex nihilo.

TEMPORARY AUTONOMOUS PUDDLE

Trefoil clover & grass drowned
in clear rain puddle assume
hypnogogic status. Mad Sweeny
would see therein a miniAtlantis or Lyonesse
chained in Time & wavering in Space
watercress beneath ecstatic rivulets
that will fill the streambeds of Hell
at the last Trump.
                            Even mud gains
gemlike nebulosity potent
with luminous sprouts & wriggling
animalcules: translucent
                   Brownian soup
to the loony's hungry eye
& lovesick appetite for humiliation.
Charged with hydrolytic energies
bubbling with negative ions
cup for saints, a bathing
of bare feet the Pope would envy
bath for sparrows
seltzer of woodsprites
entoptic & nocturnal as
                      an egg
the green spill dazzles
                   & reflects
the mayfly day.

WALLKILL

(For Robert Kelly)

Warm day after the Day of the Dead
river looks plump, cloudy cider
sparkling optimistic cornicopious
mulled w/windblown gold leaves
friend of bard & farmer—& after all
who else counts? But then dusk
gathers round like shrouds at a
                                    victorian funeral
back when death was death & not yet
hygienically tucked away. (Those
who no longer believe in witchcraft are
doomed to re-invent it under other names
& then discover themselves defenseless
against its most maleficent spells.)
Weedy & lugubrious water-maples droop
like mourners at an antique wake
sodden with whiskey & cake. Deep blue
disguised as gray suffuses the banks
& cornfields in a melancholy pall
of 19th century shadow almost
palpable as mist but ineffable.
A bloated moon, etc.
Dark side of the river: long-ago
flooded ruins of summer camp
for poor boys from Brooklyn
somewhere out in sluggish ox-bows
beneath cold pines I hear
a whippoorwill the American nightjar
an owl an unnamable rustling
in the underbrush. Who knows

what future poets suffered here, precocious
existential crises moved
by an apprehension of mourning
sorrows precious & redeemable.
Let us choose in "love of fate"
the ghosts that once chose us
out of the river that flows from
Summerland into November.

HYDROGRAPHICON

like imp of the perverse this verse
is crushing my peaches.
Invert Converts To Extraversion
Exposes Self to Convent. Hurt, the
nuns retaliate with tightly rolled black
umbrellas suddenly flexible as dried
elephant prongs. I'm the panegyrist
of filled-in canals, altho certain sections
still flow sluggish with
psychotropic water lilies. Ghost canals
may create feng-shui leylines
beneath valuable viewshed.
Can you learn how to profit
from this knowledge?

THE D&H CANAL

"Typhon makes the river dust
beating off troops of naiads
from their streamy beds, one
not so much walking on water
as tripping along it like a roadway
barefoot in flight, a watery creature.
He sucks up the creek, quick drink before dinner
the level sinks, she struggles
thrusting one foot forward then
the other along the thirsty streambed
till she's mired to her knees
in bottom prison of mud."

—Nonnos,
Dionysiaca, II/53 ff.

Under an alien regime
choked to death on brambles
Culture replaces Nature &

vice versa.
The dead lack genuine innocence
a pool of still jade, petrified tears
of a myriad Irish sub-sub-engineers
cyclopaean ruins, lost mines—
amateur archaeologists of

industrial decline
we're the authors of our own weird pulp
in a shallow trance of

sunlight deprivation
a Rosicrucianism for the Cement Age
proclaimed unfit by Eugenics.
Corn-fed & serene, Nature
draws nearer in states of decay
& must serve as

our invisible Nile.

MOUNTAIN LAKES

An infinity of plasticity suffuses the Past
w/ living craquelure, shifty, shiftless
open to the lure of every crackerjack
or cliometrician. Something endures, sure,
but scarcely facticity. Minnewaska
means nothing in good Algonkian
the water so glacially pure nothing
lives in it but mysterious salamanders
scuttling like animate runes in the
crevices of a chaotic attractor.
Evil nazi hoteliers have been exorcized by
Smoky the Bear the Orwellian mascot
of a gentle fading away into (mis)

          representation
& benthemite spleen. Princess Mohonk
reimagines herself as cynosure of eco-tourism
cheery as a girlscout—
the conundrum being that both public
& private property are theft

         semantic bear traps
for unwary hikers & hamadryads.
"Praise pays

     but not in cash."

*(Note: endquote from Greg Foster of Ikaria, "Two Months in
Myopia", unpubl. MS. 2005)*

SCENIC HUDSON

"Let me be one of the Heliades
beside the stream of mourning Eridanos
& I will drop amber
from my eyelids"
—Nonnos
Dionysiaca II/152

Sing our visit to 1911
the decayed millionaires in their
rotten mansions, when the Past
      was deeper
like compost, its
ship cemeteries, its fabulous hats
        & chokeweed.
Ghosts become real when they're written down
real but different—a
      debilitating museumization
a kind of negative hallucination
replacement of Civilization by
something else, something more dire
darker & more salvific
        "...Moose...Indians..."
   —Thoreau's last words
What's So Great About Reality?
was our slogan. We fished for eels
for coral, that prefiguration
of the Sophic Hydrolith.
Take this pill
in the form of light itself
the river's epiphanic
      doppleganger.
At supersonic velocities
the past becomes very shallow
as if seen from a bridge
the Road of Whales.

RHIZOMES

*"Why don't you white people get a
religion of your own?"*
                    —Anonymous American Indian
Poet

possible previous reincarnations flashing
past the train from Mallow to Cork,
                              a dwarfish folklorist
et fuckin cetera
in a soft green light in the late
                              Chalcolithic
maybe in the astral body
                    barbarian clouds
the bardic ritual of bacon & cream.
We got this special yoga for willing
suspension of disbelief, wellwater that will
save lave bathe & quench yr yen
for slo-mo geomantico-mesmeric fits.
Pretty soon you'll come to feel cattle
are the only true wealth, that they're
holding down the edges of the scenery
& propping up the sky
                    photographs
of fairy artifacts in Bewley's Oriental
                              Coffee House
with holes in their neoplatonic shoes & socks.
In the pub the very shadows dark as
porter in a surge of tears, the Hereditary
Piper & I pissed as newts in the
ancient mud of Wicklow, citizens of a
sunken reality that appears once every seven years
just offshore to the West. All religions
                    are Ghost Shirt Religions.

I Had Sex In Atlantis
rapt by aliens from
                    inner space
amphibian race adept at
miscegenation irrumation undinism
underwater weightless & gilled
we spilled albino caviar
                    opal spelt
in froggy streamers of albumenesque
slime. We fear no Noahchite tide
bring on the antarctic meltdown
devastating to batrachiophiles like us
                    ophiolatrists
dating back to dear dead Blavatskian days.
Let the dam bust just so long as we've
drained the glands of Neptune &
satiated our reptilian lusts.

CASTING RUNES

Assume the vatic position
stir the entrails of this tripe
this tarot of the culinarians.
Spots on the liver the original
                         emotional organ
parallel the eleven categories of
                         thunderbolts
memorialized (but lost) by
                         Etruscan augurs
—a kind of seasickness-de-siècle
has us clutching the rail heaving
prognostications or anyway premonitions
overboard like unwanted ballast.
Everyone gets a little cut of the meat.
Dracontius the last court poet of the
Vandals in their alabaster palaces in
Tunisia plumed the
fast-melting dynasty w/ epicules of mauve
& tarnished silver. Three generations of
Scythian berserking and here, w/ jasmine
stuck behind the ear, a Nordic Salammbô
rife w/ catamites & Manicheans.
Then the Byzantine fleet sweeps over our
horizon in an ecstasy of iconodulia
& inundates our brains w/ spookery. So much
for the Vandal idyll.
                         We remember the North
                           with the clarity of myth
                           we plan to travel there
                           complete with grand piano
                           if not for these jaundiced
                           Millerite forbodings of
                           boredom.

Our hyperbolic fancies waft us ever
northward over the lip of the great
Hole in the Pole discovered & suppressed
by Admiral Byrd; white is the color of mourning
                    Nomen est omen.
                    Perhaps if we change
                    our name we can
                    change our stars.

The caged bird formulates no hypotheses
how flowers come into focus when you
know their names: purple loosestrife or
joe pye weed or snowdrops like
spilled moonstone. He
has machines for his amazement.
The very bars are woven of music
down to the bone. He never marvels
how the air has ceased to tickle
& caress. Or how the flowers
sleep like fragments of mirror. Suet
& seeds arrive & shit is removed
but how or whence no caged
bird need ever enquire.

POEM WITHOUT FOOTNOTES

Certain books
you open just once & you're
damned
       like the Necronomicon.
Tunes can be haunted
& bring bad luck
          or visions
or both at once
       bad luck & visions
            at once.
The forbidden is always also the holy
so only those who risk both
can attain either. Such a book
would saturate the numinosity of its
       potential existence in space .
with a presentiality so dense as to vanish
without trace:
         heard in the ear
           heard in the air
heard in the darkness between hills
written by non-human hands.
And why not? better damned
         and/or saved
or both at once than not at all.

ON THE INDEX

Without censorship the heart blurts
secrets for nothing, birthrights
for pottage—too much yawp too much wattage
no finesse no english no backspin.
Use true names of things & they may
possess betray & leave you in lurches.
They may show teeth.
They may be part wolf. Only
the Nihil Obstat stands between me &
the abyss of clarity. Irony
is my Imprimatur. Doublespeak alone
allows this stance oblique to
all other angles. Silence is loquacious
if not eloquent. Stealth
cracks the Acme Safe of language.

GEDANKENEXPERIMENT

Fall upon each lacustrine letter
like a gourmet slurping alphabet soup
the W in water deciphers a wave
the V in wave a ripple or byte of the
hieroglyph ∧∧∧∧ pronounced N as in
Nile navigation nautilus Neptunian
appears even earlier in Ireland indecipherable
portentous as the old dream about stars
in the shape of a wolf—an example
from our archives preserved in
                              canopic jars
like pickled tripe—ergo clearly
Atlantean in origin. Sprinkle
magnet filings on taut membrane
try to make Chladni diagram
          with amplified chanting
vibrating the tympanum with
                              rosin'd bow
make watery hydrohieroglyphicographics
shaped like W's & M's & V's

∧∧∧∧∧
∧∧∧∧∧
∧∧∧∧∧

SECRETS OF THE SERAPEUM

The vast animalheaded idol's mouth
connects to a tube bored thru
temple wall to secret chamber behind
the visage where I crouch murmuring
into a funnel. Boom boom. But
the trick is I'm actually possessed—
I hear what I'm saying but can't
stop myself, faint as I am w/ fumes
of natron & burnt laurel. Lies
I tell tend to come true. The temple
is so big it has its own weather,
echoes that return hours later
with different meanings. Acoustic
anomalies cause distortions, somber
& portentous, garbled but ominous.
Afterwards when it's too late
everything will become less clear—
                              so that now
each word you hear bears double
the freight of foreboding & yet
remains pure gibberish to the
bewildered ear.

By a slight shift if would be easy
to believe crow gave us
song & not that the song
is about the crow

Instead of species we'd envision
an invisible crow behind
the ones we know who also
know us so well

thus not describe but participate
on some level beyond words
which appeal by their amuletic
value alone

as crowishness. Words themselves
shift shape, never mind bodies
or rather words *are* bodies
of sound not flesh—

crow-speech as sonic
aura of crow, halo of caw
caw, unseen bird-body
stretched to include us.

What with crow, ice, snow & sun
a collage of heraldry chartered according
to the doctrine of forged signatures at
two minutes per diem from now till St. John's Eve
cooks up occidental haikus raucous with
lumpenprole impedimenta from the telephone poles—
brainless proclamations by raven as barbarian
harbinger of just another day in the village
but suddenly naked—like those
                                    anxiety dreams
about highschool—but since one is
invisible there's no shame. It's bracing
as striding across some himalayan glacier
generating yogic heat & scattering trolls
with imperious gestures of shiny black wing.

ETHICAL BIND

Each day is the last of its kind
so plant a tree even an
American chestnut doomed to
wither & vanish like the roast
chestnut vendors of yore or the
honey bee. And even if
you plan to live forever
plant a tree as if each day
were your last—which
from the point of view of
November 2005 is
true. A century from now
if there is a century from now
no one will ask if you
paid your bills or returned
your calls but someone might
be there in the forest to hear
your tree when it falls.

Not everyone's lucky enough to have
lived thru the 1890s. I have them
in my dry bones
backlit day-glo
peacocks & purple birthdays
                              long
portentous nitrous oxide dream that evades
pen & paper & leaves behind mere
collectable ephemera
                         shoebox crammed
w/ embarrassing playbills yellowing erotica
the bitter mouth of a terminal hangover
mildew of dead books
like dealing patience w/ an old tarot
in which the stains & creases
mean as much as the faded trumps.

PEAR CIDER

Nothing compares to watching a slice
of the cusp between August & September
drift by w/ wilted & riverine
                        in-betweenness
algae on the marsh & herons on the march
fallen black walnuts smelling of
                        expensive soap
drinking pear cider in some
sylvan reserve "nestled", as
realestatists say, beyond the reach
of weed-whackers.
                        Ancient civilizations come
to value these evanescent
                        untransmissible
little epiphanies over the grander
                        grimmer
peaks of history & passion. But ours
is an age grown old too quickly that
learned these lessons a bit too late.

WHAT EXACTLY
IS
JOE PYE WEED?

Ignore the handbooks don't trust the locals
nothing remains but to drag
every reader into the swamp
some August & point.

The dead mailman
from the Dead Letter Office
steams open my envelopes &
steals my dead letters
lifting heavy wax seals with
razor blade & then replacing them
intact.
  How to prove that I knew you then
when artifacts lack all trace?
no lingering scent no silk ribbon?
not even amnesia?
    Outer Space Aliens
would at least leave memory lesions
behind them like dogs that don't bark
or brainwashed assassins waiting unknowingly
for letters of intent
that were never sent.

How local is a breeze?
Will this June ripple reach
from here to Connecticut? Did it
first arise in China? Or
just across the river in the unborn
corn? It's the sheer scale of it all
that's hard to grasp. Our catbird
for instance: has this raga
been going on since the Upper Jurassic
in a family of Bachs that's out-
lasted Mt. Qaf? In effect
an immortal catbird? Or
a breeze that leaves
no trace.

CATALPA

(poème trouvée, *Webster's*)

Modern Latin direct from
AmerInd (Creek) "head with wings".
Seeing catalpa bloom—blam—
transforms hot humid day
into sexual thrill
Seraphim's limbs
boughs cut into bows
from proto-Shinto
magicians of Ch'u
(see Waley's *Nine Songs*)
already lamenting loss
of amorous contact with
disembodied spirits.

Have you noticed certain fruit trees
on the 2 or 3 days they blossom
w/ insistent bees shimmering in place
even without a breeze
Van Goghish halo's in arborial throes
of vegetal orgasm
                          or considered
thunderstorms as actual rather than
merely allegorical you-know-what
stroking earth with wet fingers
till bolts spark up & down from
primal soup to nuts
                          like a panorama
in the Hall of Dinosaurs: Gaia
in unspeakable infantile arousal
so primal as to symbolize only itself.

(for Jake)

We need a
source of bioluminescence
such that mixed w/ water would
serve as invisible ink
legible only in darkness
calligraphic will-o-the-wisps
or crushed fireflies
fungal spores spun to a
bright frenzy by
spagyric lore of the
raven that resembles a
writing desk because of its
inky plumes. Sun at midnight's
no mere metaphor but
metaphosphor
our lampblack
our squid.

Cults that last for a very long time
accrete veridical patinas of barnacles
dendrochronologically. Like the yew they
immortalize themselves by sucker roots, air roots,
even when the original trunk long dead
rots away leaving a hollow column for owls or bats.
Old churchgrounds were not planted with yews just
because yews symbolize rebirth & immortality—
churchyards were planted around already-ancient yews
because yews ARE immortal, & continually reborn
some in England & Ireland said to be at least 6000 years old
evergreen with red berries said to be psychotropic
or poisonous (often the same thing). What psychonaut
will return with news from that druidic fane?

CODEX PLUVIAE

Everything we want is in that garden
including the idea of the garden
like bubbles of rain riding the river's face
& shutting out the war
the war that's over before it begins.

Little jewels dug up in dreams
allées of laurel & privet
permanent as rain
that is to say, permanent while it lasts.
Back to the Nineteenth Century
like wet dogs. Like idealists.
Remember those foot-pedaled "Swan Boats" of the 1950s?
Or was that someone elses's memory?

We're angry at everything we know
& we know everything. Maybe our drugs
are wiping out whole banks of precious data—
what a relief. Down topiary rows
                            blurred with mist
where we can't see them: ghosts, or maybe tour guides
in period costume, drifting away from us
urgent but inarticulate, pressing on our sleep
deeper in the maze, closer to sundial or gnomon
closer to the payload, the June afternoon
the place of the kiss that's never given
except in books.

Growing still under quick puddles
of drinkable rain: drowned origami landscapes
you could stare at them forever
& become a different self, younger,
perhaps more serious.

Take a bleak loading dock
behind a bankrupt superstore
somewhere in the Mall Zone late
one night in the decline of Time
an absence compared to which the
presence of the most guignol
vampire might seem positively
heimlich
a place where nothing human has ever
died
    or lived
           yet or ever will
where a single
ragged chicory blooming thru concrete
provides the only potential death
to touch this unhaunted vacuum with breath.

The lure of raw brut outsider art
lurks in its absence from Culture & History
hence no Holocaust no Curse of Adorno
a romanticization of insanity sometimes
connived at by the mad themselves
"barking mad I tell you"
like a pheasant pretending a wound
dragging a broken wing away from her
admittedly badly hidden nest.

Birds believe in the
imminence of rain
                            & also its
eminence &
immensity. Do I
mean this literally?
                            Deo volente
& once & for all eternity
                            fuck Descartes.

When comes the next swan-boat?
pedallo à deux into the terminal dusk
of the final edwardian serpentine
white mainline hit of magnolia
crk-creak crk-creak slowly into shadows
of weeping willows. Real swans, startled,
heave themselves aloft
                      an aerostatic miracle
hurl heavily overhead in vast pinion-whoosh
unheard outside some German
                         Expressionist horror
                                flick.

AGGRONAUT

Picture them sitting around. Someone says
y'know, whoever could come up with a
                              seedless watermelon
could really rake in the dough, no?
And here we are today: a triumph
of American know-how: the end of all
grinning kids in seedspitting duels.
Once it was the African flag: green red black but
now no more black. Could've kept it in a tub
of ice-house ice under the porch
but what's the point, eh? Now the product
chews like plastic tastes like Nutra-Sweet
& lacks not only seeds but water.
I see them now, sitting around, those
                              agroindustrialists
dead & burning in the pits of hell.

Vegetables undergo slow but observable
                    tumescence w/ bland pretense
of effortlessness—or at least
                    one hopes so.
Farmers across the river are
                    stoning the crows
by remote control w/ a
                    robot shotgun
blast every two minutes like a sick headache
bang! the supersaturated atmosphere
startles our crow-cousins from the corn.
I confess to corvinesque aspects
glossy blackness
                    roadkill gourmandise
various burglaries &
                    shapeshifting tendencies
bourgeois bargain basement Raven
                    w/ yellow'd eyes
peeling away the pretenses of those
                    agroindustrial dolts.
Not in my name! Not in my name!
Who cares? They'll have their war
                    without you.

OLD INDIA HANDS

(for Shiv)

1.

India can be an albatross to a
writer's career
     too exotic too Beat
passé heavy on the sleeper's chest
& insufficiently post-colonial—
        a bacillus
you never kick
     a little monsoon cloud
that hovers over yr head & follows you
from novel to novel like mildew
or bookworms (the original proponents
of hypertextuality). Our opium.
Our live-in Cornell box. Some corner
of a forgotten skull that is forever
Hindoostan, priest-ridden stoned to the gills
& flashing on a monstrous case of déja vu
that wipes out suburban 1950s New Jersey
         like the plague.

2.

This "Ganesh Brand" acts as Proustian madeleine
evoking misspent youth far from the Seine
or Hudson for that matter: farther away
under spreading banyan trees we
hippies lounged & smoked our weedy bidis.
Benares made us what we are today
relics lost as any Vanished Raj, we
maunder on w/ anecdotes quite dodgy
re: hash deals, VD, O-dens & religion
steam trains, morphine doctors & a smidgen
of dysentery, sadhus, Khumbamelas
Parsis, Jains et al.—exotic fellas
with exotic flaws & foibles on display
like flashers with elephantiasis
or being/consciousness/bliss
until—to shut us up—you'd gladly pay.

Escapism = Resistance
drifts toward the mythic
implausible like a dirigible blown
with nitrous oxide finally so
attenuated that spirals of
incense can trance us
with streaming sensations of thinking
we remember what it was.

Wet streets
        gain a certain self-importance
                in the evening
suggesting lofty goals too lofty
& thus paradoxically a
             logistical retreat.
Think of this rain
as a medium of communication
               between us
slick & black as asphalt
but moving slowly as a warm front
into the cold of any distance
              between us
as if you lived just over the river
& words could swim
           but instead
are curried back into the funk of
Not Yet—still
monadic but with a modicum
of gemütlichkeit.

HARMONIAL INSTASONNET

Ambiguity
        (I forget the number)
                        as when
an object changes color according to angle
of light like moiré silk or alexandrite.
                                D'Annunzio
proposed a constitution based on music. Fourier
suggests scent as pivot of the senses.
Flee the world for a start. Dawn
would be another example, white
as the shoulder of Pelops. Lacking
clear identity it can never become
an image of itself. Real but
                        unquantifiable
(like ESP) it mingles sewage & benzoin
skunk & jasmine, vile & sublime &
specializes in the sidelong glance
in the supermarket aisle.

NON-JURING INSTASONNET

Deceased in reduced circumstances
the Pre-Adamite Hermaphrodite
                         could read Pindar
                  in the original.
In the Vestry, soiled lace, Vespers.
Bruised light from the clerstory.
Laudanum compounded by spagyria.
Don't waste fading twilight on doctrine
                  subject to infinite schism.
How we wish we'd banned the telephone
in 1905 in a bid to retain our
Anglo-Irish heritage & inherent
                         sadness.
I've visited the very street
north of the Liffey with its decrepid
Georgian facades
now extremely rare (not seen except
in crepitations of déjà vu).

Primitive roses? primordial roses? or just prim?
Huge architectural sets of flowering blackberries
sit dripping like landed UFOs
but I can't get the Japanese effect
shadowy forms in rubber boots
chasing bullfrogs where the creek is swollen
buzzing around me, pressing my face
into wet blossoms
                    "Unspeakable Cults".

So the Devil is the perfect monotheist
the perfect lover. Someday all this
                              will be ours
everything but the heraldic sable
& embrace of darkness.

STARRY WISDOM SECT
TRACT #21

In the end times we retreat to a cubic
iron walled fortress somewhere above the
arctic circle. "Will you have a spot of tea?"
"Yes my dear I think I'll join you."
Everything reduced to its platonic archetype
& we discover we don't like it. What
to do? When I hear the phrase "sustainable
development" I wish I had a luger to
reach for. Swamp Angel Swamp Angel
we've seen the last of you & yr happy dog
like an almanac from an unused year
or the tingling enjoyable fright of a
darkened planetarium. Don't put
a name to it & no one will ever even see it.

Verse is burglary
        with printing press as fence
stealing what it can't afford to buy
or keep & offing it for mere pence
on the pound to some shady pawnshop
of the emotions. All the gems in
Salomé have slipped thru its
soapy fingers—all the vintages
courtesans & little private suppers
of a Balzacian villain—enough bolts of silk
to smother a Court Eunuch in
ecstatic mummification—and all
for the thrill of breaking & entering
by night & fingering some frozen
climax of pearls or cracking the safe.

A DAY'S WORK FOR YVAN GOLL

Our taste for flowers & certain gems
anything gnarly or excessively chaste
                              has helped us
to escape so cleverly by flickering
                              out of existence
about the same time as the Ottoman Caliphate.
Before we realized it we were the Temporary Pope.
I lost my head for a day & an angel
with heavy wings hung over me. But now
that I can see myself in the mirror again
                              no trace lingers.
Pass it around like a hot potato, this papacy.
By an odd coincidence one sip of the green fairy
will prolong our reign by minutes—
the wan wand will fall to another hand
like a gold ring found beneath the pillow
after dreaming of a chemical marriage.

(Note: Yvan Goll was appointed by Apollinaire as second "pope"
of surrealism, but was displaced by Breton. This sonnet marks
the temporary revival of Gollist Surrealism.)

Real shepherds don't write pastoral hexameters
but so what? Closeness to Nature is a
kind of ambulatory schizophrenia—but
do we care? Observers & collectors
of impressions & sylvan vaguenesses we
play an axial role perhaps even soteriological
as savers of phenomena & savors
of humus & rot—ineffable but collective
saviors of all discarded & redundant
tastes—aesthetic witnesses
to the evanescence of agrarian populism
—poets as iconographists of decay
helpless as figures in a classical landscape
but ever ready to share the blame.

JANUS

resolves to inhale more snowflakes
trace more fallen stars to roost
cause more uproar in the Invisible World
hoping to precipitate showers of
                             demoralizing rain
over metropolitan areas
                             to boost all
work with weather (that terminal monster The
Revenge of the Pathetic Fallacy) and
learn to live in mid-air the last possible Outside
like Finnish weather wizard in
tesseractoid airship armed with anti-
deadly orgone cannon to burst & disperse
psychotextual miasmas & radioactive attitudes
from altitudes where atmosphere grows thinner
but more bracing than the most exquisite sin.

" 'AIR-QUOTES' "

It's an ugly gesture & meant to be
like a stinking use of irony around
irony itself. If History signifies the long
wriggle to escape from History
then History does indeed seem to have
come to an End in the sense of
having no end, like a Mall designed
by Ballard or Baudrillard: Piranesian
Carceri distended into Escheresque dimensions
of cybershopping, teleologic Moebius strips of
WalMarts, multiplex'd vistas
in which whatever it was you wanted
infinitely recedes at a speed to match
yr credit rating, including death.

(Note: In viva voce performance the title can be
announced simply by making the gesture.)

DOVE-O-GRAM

Muse-abandoned drivel
compulsive logorrhea
mail-order scam with myself
as addressee, two million dollars
in a suitcase in Nigeria, late
2nd century forgery—& still I
believe O Lord in a lost envelope
of forgotten directions to my
waking self, an anaesthetic
revelation drained of all significance
hence endowed with delphic darkness
an organ of prosody camouflaged
as an organ, a letter from
someone who remembers me.

ISLAND

jewel of light in a bezel of light
air creaks with light
& iodine skreeks of gulls:
breeze from the Lost Continent of MU
                              dispels
the cloud of ghosts

seduction of absence
luxe of disvestment
sandy eros of this nowherescape
fulltime summer camp sketched
                    in a few colors
gray rain monotony sanctity
clouds like heavenly hosts.

SEMI-AUTOMATIC TEXT

Incubo-succubism on a higher plane—
we could cite a full panoply of turkish delights
too deliberate for daylight—angels with
                              nocturnal remissions
will receive our aspergillations & lustrations
along with the usual greco-mesopotamian
line-up of suspects & freemasonic bric-a-brac
for frazerian bricoleurs. We like it all
because it's VAGUE—
                    Love Bowers on the Astral Plane
where everything is bottle-green, elf-shot
with corruscading color organ glissandos,
a shower of Salamanders & Undines who
invade the Catskills but just beyond the
pale of crude appearances, all of them with
superb mustachios neatly waxed yet somehow
Old Testament, translucent as hothouse
orchids in the parlor w/ its horsehair sofas &
portraits in oval frames backed w/ dried ferns
or palmfronds from the Holy Land—player piano
accompanied by spirit trumpet—a tawdry
hierogamy at the top of a makeshift
                              ziggurat.

PLANCHETTE

There's a song in my heart but not my head
Pity most spiritualist automatic writing turns out
$\qquad\qquad\qquad\qquad$ so dull
as if the dead had nothing to say—or anyway
nothing we haven't heard before.
$\qquad\qquad\qquad\qquad$ Perhaps
writing itself began as a sneaky way
of letting the dead speak in dead letters
words without breath words without a face
"dead fingers talk"
$\qquad\qquad\qquad$ & space is abolished.
I can't get down to the song
it's buried with the dead. In May
or June it re-appears as a bush
& says I saw the goddess naked.
Trumpets will float above the medium's cabinet
telling us what to think in the perfect dark.

Winter is our politics
          of separatism. Winter
cuts off high passes
isolates our xenophobic valleys.
Winter is a crazy relative locked
in the attic, spawn of Dagon.
Winter is vaguely menacing & reactionary.
Incestuous trailer trash
white as ice. Lost colony
of albinos. Up in the frozen hills
we mutter about secession.
North the sacred direction.
Our policy of global cooling,
our reindeer, our toadstools,
          our zoning violations.

Suddenly the door bursts open
the room is invaded by a posse
of philosophes in snuff-colored velvet
w/ doilies round their stiff necks
& the rattle of coffee cups.
Everything now turns the color of mud
like bad Rembrandt. Perfect freedom
means perfect surveillance
a panopticon of vapid acedia
                    the encyclopaedists decide.
Cosmonauts Report No Signs of Heaven.
A machine that erases space, the room
becomes an airport lounge where the philosophes
doze fitfully in their plastic chairs
masters of anywhere—but who cares?

"Ye sons of Indolence
do what you will"
—James Thomson

Hero of my own gothick novel
apiaries corncribs lightning-rods
my own Gnostic fragment:
rotting redbrick factories
abandoned stinking canals
Chas Addams mansions mouldering along
the Raritan River
cankers of the spirit on the bland
smiling face of heroic modernism.
I'm having difficulties with dematerialization
I can't feel my feet
I'm bowled over by anaesthetic revelations
like a Dutch nine-pin.
The brain has forgotten this alien abduction
but my molecules remember.

ARKTOS

(for Joscelyn Godwin)

Cold is conservative fire is progressive
bread speaks in runic shapes
not quite letters not quite words
summer is nature winter is culture
where the police can't reach us
till the weather clears

Summer is Neolithic, French, downtown
Winter is Paleolithic, German, uptown
here in the tower safe from telepathic rays
cocoon'd in dreams like moths or sloths
couldn't we dare to dabble in forbidden notions
like Naturopathy? Nudism? Neanderthal Lib?

or Jukes-&-Kallikaks tri-racial isolate
in-bred freakish but alluring hillfolk
who keep to dark hollows & follow old ways
that would make H.P. Lovecraft kvell with
frissons of eldritch disgust or lust, that
aging aesthete with pinn'd pupils & irises
the color of Finnish weather wizard's washed-out
icy blue marbles, nodding, nodding
cold & reactionary.

COARSENED MIRACLES

They save up tears in canopic jars
like royal entrails then slip spoonsful
past our lips w/ mournful expressions hinting
it's somehow our fault if the gates of prophecy
are sealed like gummy eyelids.
Break-throughs are treated as break-ins, burglaries
in the Mall of Dead Faiths.
The book is a paper hoop & as
you read a sudden tiger leaps thru

                             —crash!

a kung-fu fist thru page direct to jaw
comic stars, whizzing planets—
theophany has its slapstick moments
with slight variations
like ears or snowflakes.

TO ARTAUD
(for Clayton Eshleman)

Let me say what I truly think for once
even if it has to be translated into
Latvian or Lettish or Icelandic to ensure
no cop sees it in my own languageland
or at least smudge it raggedly
with enigmatisms, rodomontades
bad smells blind alleys & acrostics
so none but adepts who've completed
our mail-order course & received
                                    their decoder rings
can ever digest this feuilleton
                    this blatt
or fiery flying roll of flagrant
            augustinian confessionalism
                    & stolen pears

besides, who cares?—another Artaud clone
babbling decorticated dabbling
in electroshocking diablérie
                                    o no
free speech belongs only
to those who are never heard
or if heard never believed
or if believed then only
in prisons for the criminally insane
by fellow loons & ogres

and I a louse in yr coat, Artaud
a parasite riding on yr reputation
for meaningless blather.

LOST GOSPEL

Time is eschatological but space is
soteriological. Turn yr back, walk out
shake the dust of Time's ideas from the
heels of space. "Alien Was Father Of My Child":
a light-skinned green, like chlorophyll & cream:
Leonardo da Vinci on DMT
slick, wet, reptilian, encased in
a caul of ectoplasmic slime—
the true secret messiah appears
an image worthy of Dali at his worst
plunges our heads beneath the salty
river of warm tears & excrement
redeemed. But only in the text.
Turn in all those coupons
you've been saving for one moment
of disdain.

BAD WINTER

Dark ice
  dank ice
    negative window
thru which we watch our books & papers
drifting back into the Past, a
nauseating congealation
     orphans frozen in the snow
pompes funèbres
    & bitter reminiscences.
The Poetry Police
  will have none of this pathetic
    moralization of nature
angels receding
  deeper into Winter as
    Endtime allegory;
only the direct & most alarming religion
will answer the question "How long
    has this been going on?"
Note that Saturn rules both aspects
"Time's Arrow"
"Second Law"
"Saving Remnant"
So?
  Once again we retire to our cellars
for the long American sub-zero winter
burning our books behind us.

"NATURE POET"

can barely tell one bird from another
—no John Burroughs (more likely
                          William S. or Edgar Rice)
loves other peoples' gardens park-strolls
                              & distant panoramas
viewshed from upstairs window
         full of fog as cup with tea
                         or democratic ghosts.
Eureka
reactionary as some tribal elder
                         whose sacred mountain
was levelled for a parking lot
                         two hundred years ago
full of resentment as an egg with meat
yet featureless as the sea
                         distracted
from Basho's pines & snow
                         ultimately false
as that which they oppose
                         & yet
more important than truth.
Satisfying the jones for ozone
& the smell of melting mud
is all about as natural as
                    Marie Antoinette
as shepherdess or Yeats in the
                    garden at Coole
in fact
         downright cruel.

194

WINTER IN AMERICA

"Community is more than just people"
I learn while waiting on hold
from smarmy robotessa voice backed by synth
soothing as intravenous drip.
"Community means eldercare"
& something that sounds like "pet therapy".
The tape rewinds & plays again & still
it sounds like "pet therapy".
Days are closing in, as some character
says in some glum Anglo-Irish
Big House novel. Soon snow
will come & shelter us
                    in narrative.

DOSSIER

The invisible childhood friends
the talking dogs
seemingly random placements
of anomalous objects
in the landscape of language
cause dreams so subtly disturbing
so intricately foreboding that in fact
no one remembers them.
                        Cushlamachree!
day's dazzle makes us want to leap
but only mentally
                  or turn our coats
inside-out or upside-down
like déclassé intelligentsia
& sell all our paltry secrets
to a non-existent USSR.

(thanx to Crockett Johnson's
"Barnaby & Mr O'Malley")

(for Sandy Seaton)

Cold Mountain
could've been a kind of
        nickel-&-dime nirvana
like the Farmer's Almanac
w/ column-fillers by Basho—
the whole bleak yet
amorous ice-capade of
solsticial sadness up there
not five miles away by
astral projection—
Cold Mountain seen from my
kitchen window rising above the
red dust of electromagnetic soup.
Han Shan
paid in loneliness & depression
no doubt for his few moments
of literary satori
               not to mention
the no-cal zen diet like
Mad Sweeny's watercress.
                  Juke Zen
you might call it—busted
for camping w/out a permit
threatening property values by washing
his socks in the creek
sent to a Home where he can
cool his heels & try for
enlightenment on thorazine.

Serious books
float like miniature icebergs
                    past my window
slowly grinding to a nordic halt
                    of jammed floes
right under my nose
& all their authors like
                    little eskimos
leap up trying to sell me
                    their blubber.
But perverse as Nebuchadnezzar I
persist in browsing
                    insubstantial
salads of bitter herbs.

Winter just portentously left the room
a moment ago
                slammed the door
                            plunged
the rest of the cast in glum
silence & is now banging around
outside flinging garbage cans &
sluicing away Spring's first
                      road kill.
Even shrill peepers are stilled
by this mud bonanza, chilled
to their delicious legs.
                  A tiny toast
to the Thimble Theater, a subtle
                      sublethal sip of its
noxious toxic but adorable pop.
                          Pay per view.
Permanent Brain Damage (PBD)
is surely not too high a price
for the lubricious Lilliputians & their
mini-Tijuana circus. Popeye as Populist
or Priapus sprays the mountains w/ his
viscid spue
            —so well-drawn—
                        spawn
of Iblis as I am on rainy days
of entheogenic dew.

SUBLIMATION

Subliminality
up to the lintel
the limen the limit
a distillation of solids
like smoke escaping from the tent
thru the hole in the roof
into some literally higher solid
crystalline & odoriferous—
like saving coupons
for papal indulgences.
                   And who's
the sublimate the sublimation or
simply the Sublime in this equation?
                       Are mere words
like drops squeezed from rocks or tears
of the oyster robbed of its nacreous
excrements? Are we still laboring
under the 19th century image of consciousness
as some kind of choo-choo train?
like Houdini making an
               elephant disappear?

To smell & taste the true spices
cinnamon clove nutmeg pepper ginger
is to want to give back some of that
too-much to the spirits who must be
tutelary to such trees. Instantly
the relevant islands appear to yr
pineal eye where Javanese esotericism meets
Dyak headhunter shamanism w/ vegetation
that smells like gongs sound &
demonic bells ting tong to bring
such fruits to fruition. Only
a culture of deep trance could've
ever deserved or survived living in
proximity to such powerful tastes.

Welcome to the roadside chapel
my concrete garden my Elagabalus feast
where the grapes are synthetic amethysts
don't break yr teeth! a garden of monsters
where it seems Our Savior
                                            never breathed
hushed stilled & waiting
in the off-season chill
stifled by your lack of faith
your inability to pray
your creaky knees
                          Welcome
to my Druid Grove theme-park, its
                                    plaster megaliths
& fake oaks hung with tacky crystals
like cold rain.
                      Don't drive by
you'll remember all yr life
the Virgin made of broken bottles
the plastic mistletoe, the
weird piped-in organ music & the feeling
you were somehow expected.

WE SHALL NOT BE MOVED

To live on the premiss that
to live on the premisses hic et nunc
yes even in squalid orgies of presentiality
& fetishistic topophilia
plumb loco for localismo
sedentary in the sediment of sentiment
sporting what phrenologists would call an
eminent bump of Adherence to the Here
would demand a georomantico-existentialist
collapse into Irrealism so pointy
& exigent as to strike all bien-pensant
secular humanist bourgeois scum
a nightmare blow & dolorous stroke
of eco-terrorist revanchist re-enchantment.

LO

O Charles Fort where're yr phenomena
gone, vanished into X-File re-runs & super
market tabloids just when we really need
at least a UFO to reassure us the Irreal
still exists & even rivals the dreary
all-too-real. Film itself is a kind of
haunting & may replace ghosts with the
absence of ghosts. Certainly one can be
$\qquad\qquad$ haunted by an absence.

Like brick through plate
glass window we're about to
launch a thought bubble with
meteoric streaming locks &
                              swift feet
as if the scent of wet wool
had a mind of its own.
Alone in our atelier
we cld open the roof & let rain
rain in to etch the plates
& print with rain instead of ink
as when Antonin Artaud
took the ferry to Dublin &
wandered around in the rain all night
& lost his magic walking stick.

Bluebells or a closely related species
glow in tree shadows incandescing
like a gas ring set on low
that gives off coolth not warmth.
I'd like to run away from my life
to somewhere like this but unfortunately
I already live here.
The common winter aconite
if blown up to twenty times its size
would fascinate Nero Wolfe or J.-K. Huysmans
with its poisonous fin-de-siècle vim.
Tiny devas do victorian dances
down there but up here in the mesocosm
everything turns to shit as per usual.

GRANGE HALL

In the applejack dusk
Progress has not blessed them
Pomona Ceres & Demeter
the Crones salute the flag.
They know the death of bees
"That's Capitalism!"
the sagging white hall
glows like bone
the hymns have untuned it.
In the starry dark
it seems logical
on the road back from
Eleusis in the
honey-thick night.

ROGUE HOLLOW

Recalcitrant cacagenic backbush squatters
halfbreed hermits witchladies & basketweavers
86'd from Arcadia banished to Bedlam
for the forest's health. But does the rattler
show gratitude or the crane cast its vote
no they're just there like air & don't care
how much money & power it takes to
comb the woods of human vermin till Earth smiles
gratefully overgrown w/ gracious nature tenaciously
regaining its sway up the Vernoykill
where everything slides into dying sighs
heavy with the "skry" "skry"
of birds predicting rain
blurring all stone walls & ruined cellars
like faded tattoos on an aging sailor.

IDOL TEARS

In the late 18th & early 19th century
people used to burst into tears
collected in chrystal phials
ancient glass stained lilac with
absorbed time
                    imparting faint scent
to the liquid
                    of languid sentiment.
Evaporation sublimates
these droplets to a dessicate
exudation or whiff of white lies
white violets pressed in albums
but like the blood of St Januarius
sometimes they re-liquify.

CHEAP WEATHER

Money, like Nature, lacks the personal touch
the landlord or the worm, dead is dead
The Social Darwinists were right, but none survived
WAR DECLARED but only in your head.
Last bit of wilderness that can't be mapped
the monster from the Id, the perfect storm
Stay tuned for the Manichean Weather Report
the nihilism of the easily bored.
Après moi le déluge, live at five
go take the dog for its shot of novocaine
les neiges d'antan, OK, but who
expected a Future with so many hurricanes?
Short-term memory loss, at easy rates:
Under the skin of the world, one suffocates.

BIG GODZILLA PSEUDOSONNET
ON CHARACTER AS FATE

Battle with the unconscious, you usually lose
sleep past banking hours
               misplace the files
on the street visualize true shapes
of people in the Unseen World.
The All-Bacon All-Marijuana Diet lets
everything ooze through or percolate upwards
               like sewage in a landfill
(if shit smelled like magnolias
                   & tuberoses)
a marsh-fill of knock-out drops
a tide of codeine syrup
               stained with violets:
wrestling with the Jacobite Angel of the unconscious
like Gorgeous George vs Man Mountain Moon
               on black-&-white TV
everyone's favorite monsters from the blue lagoon
vertiginous as the Wild Mouse at Coney Island
& far more inevitable than death or taxes.

Islands lost in time & pulp. Reincarnated Atlanteans
constitute a growing market niche.
Our ship the black schooner.
Give me a team of frogmen
& a dark & stormy night accessible
only by rainslick sheeptrack. Oceanic light
breaks over white cumulus vast as a pocket cosmos.
We'll stagger home at two AM in rubber boots—
                                    a Taoist love nest.
Attract shady offshore banking. Our Bermuda
                          pineal gland of the Atlantic.
Speak a strange patois—laughter from far away
from a Past that never actually happened.
The true treasure hidden on Treasure Island
is Treasure Island—a Saturnian Thule
beyond all price.

Amanita muscaria. Amateur musicales.
Mummery. Bundling. Hearth. Heart.
Blind harpists. Hivernation. A full-length
                              sable coat.
Stars like albino caviar in some vodka-induced
                              Black Sea
the North like a golem looms toward us
& we'll go forth to meet it like the Sabbath
with Saturnian hymns. The last grapes
will freeze solid as amethysts & then
melt into an Ice Wine sweet & blue as
December's empty sky. Holly ivy mistletoe
human sacrifices—what have we got now
to rival this seriousness? What stars?
Let's think our way into the hearts of old pines
in a cold slow implosion of nordic satori.

JACK FROST
AS ANARCHIST

My heart's in the Irish Catskills where
ice spells out words in Ogham in
crystals of dew. The very old & very young
unite in ridicule of bourgeois convention.
Xtianity itself is invaded by Frazerian delirium
                           & Norse Balderdash.
Panarcticism. World Ice Theory. Altaic Pansophism.
Our Vedic Home at the North Pole.
Beaches literally littered with amber
under the sign of the Winter King & Queen of Bohemia
those Rosicrucian runaways. Picture them (1620)
fleeing in a white sleigh drawn by white
horses—draped in ermine cloaks—a starry night.
Grande Epoque Ice Palace snowmen with icicle
                                  erections
skating by torchlight across the frozen floor
                          of a glacier.

CODE DUELLO

Nights belong to the djinn & the dogs
& everyone spends most of the day as well
immured in stone towers that squat the
                                    lycanthropic landscape
no electricity no indoor plumbing no police
                                    no McDonald's.
Whenever I read about Albania
or the Hatfields & McCoys I
try to summon up some
bien-pensant nausea at the atavistic
                    notion of revenge.
Let it be prose
                broken up
                            into uneven lines
& other such merde.
                    The whole idea
of steganography is magic
                            & all such codes
must be read with mormonesque spec's
lest the Profane etc. etc.—and
those you can have for nothing.

MY FORMER LIFE AS A VISUAL PUN

I was a man of vegetables & fruit
grape eyes banana nose cauliflower ears
green rebus jolly giant nobleman of Prague
in its brief Rosicrucian winter.
I sweated sweet slightly rotten perfumes
overripe pears & the hot melon of my forehead
the spring onions of my hair
& peeled cucumber of my tongue—

                                    and you
I suppose were made of flowers & jewels
similes taken literally
coral antimony smoke pearls rosebuds etc.
obscene white moonflowers etc.
you smelled of snow which is the odor of gems
& breathed with the orchid of your mouth.
We knew Erasmus Darwin's Vegetal Amour
anthers stamens pistils w/ attendant bees
& the bees also became parts of us
eyebrows perhaps or blush of public dust.
Then came the Defenestration
the collapse of Dee's Plan & demise
of political hermeticism
the Botanical Gardens bombed to shit
in the 30 Years War.
We died into seed
& were stored for four centuries
in canopic jars till now
if you plant us we'll rise again
lycanthropes who change into mulberries
violets & peaches rather than wolves
golems molded not of clay
but pollen.

216

TINTINABSOLUTISM

Our music must be campanological
unelectrified but louder than any amplified artificiality
pealing & plangent in the humidity of summer's armor
& draw djinn like moths to heavy curtains
bells of seven metals that can change weather
protect us from the lightning that flickers
this evening like a defective moon
baroque glissandi, the same old Holocene waterfall cascading
sparkling from the steeple campanile acting on atavistic
associations of metallurgy & alchemy in tumbling octaves
of planetary tinctures summoning stellate archons
from other dimensions
                              so that
lone strollers lovers kids on bicycles
in the aimless gloaming will fall absolute prey
to our unconscious attempt to disenlighten the torpid
leaf-heavy celestial azure with sonic dreams
                              of sleeping geniuses.

PSYCHIC NOMADISM

6000 years of cuneiform & shit
have buried the barbarians too soon
the tinker's wagon in the knacker's yard
a pile of fecal bile & psychic sludge

the tourist & the terrorist as twins.
Why choose this strip-mall over that?
crisscrossed with highways, mapped from outer space
a text-based life, the closure of the West

consumed but never lived, no smell no taste
no season, weather, grazing, music, milk
our rootless cosmopolitan is stumped
by fastfood cities sinking into waste.

A temporary nomad zone explored
but only in the land of hungry ghosts—
homeless cranks, dead hobos, crusty punks
don't constitute a true Barbarian Horde.

The plan of Gengiz Khan—burn, pillage, raze
the cities to a pyramid of skulls
till earth grows featureless as sea
at last withdraws its parasitic gaze.

The animals return in sacred time
a prairie will restore itself at last
a Scythian mummy turns up in the ruins
& shakes Von Humboldt from his dusty shelves

Connecticut assumes a desolate air
yr Wild Boys on the move—the wire clipped
the herds roam free. Is this the end
the urban Armageddon? Will we care?

TOR

Sometimes a tower is just a tower
innocent as a cigar & anyway
what's wrong with living in a lingam

with moat to cut us off from
electromagnetism, a way of looking
down, a function of writing?

Singular interlocutors are envisioned
the trained raven the dénoument—
but bones are not nothing

& every night we descend to caverns
beneath the Pole Star, ancestral
skulls our xylophone.

From these slits we can pour
boiling oil or shit down on our enemies.

There's nothing supernatural about the
hermaneutic that simply betrays it &
turns it into nasty shimmering gelatinous gray aspic
like severed fingers in a rigid consommé
or the stalker's laff-track that
punctuates yr sit-com like
spit from the balcony. And as an
added attraction it's INTERACTIVE.
You could plotz. You could punk & rot
while it continued to blink & hum
like a UFO on steroids—unless
you forget to pay the bill—O then
you're up to yr bloomin knickers
in a silence that could pass for shit.

We miss the Ice by candlelight—
this DNA is the Devil's ladder.
Clamber ruthlessly down to recover lost/found
clear memories of the Glacial
down the double spiral staircase down
the tower struck by lightning
where gnomes & giants still
inhabit linguistic substructures
& the cellars of the Dordogne—
lands beneath deep pools & springs
that connect underground to the
Ocean of Narrative. Our red hair
is the taint. Our blood type. Our
hatred of Civilization.

UNTAXED GOODS

The smuggler's cave connects by winding stairs
with the crypt of a lonely church above the cliff
the cave itself accessible only by sea—
a hidden cove too small for any but
the skinniest boat to slip in late at night
in moonless murk of phosphorescent mist.
A snake of men is winding up the beach
in boots or bare feet, cutlasses & rings
dark clothes, smudged faces. A black lamp
clutched by the hunchback parson lights their way
beneath the cave-mouth frowning in the rain.
Each smuggler lugs a cask of brandy, wine
opium or haschisch—each oval barrel
maybe three foot long & two foot wide—
upon his shoulder up into the grotto
where piles of them are stacked along with bales
of stolen silk & chests of china tea.
Now lurid flickering torches dipped in pitch
illuminate a scene of revelry—
living nightmares of the Excise Man
passing round a gold communion cup
& spilling cognac down their bristly chins:
non-violent pirates out to cheat the State's
tyrannical monopolies—to smoke
their pipes as independent lords of night
chivalric champions of the Popular thirst
& belted earls of anarchic enterprise.
The church of course is said to host a ghost
that walks on foggy nights & blinks & moans
& carries a child's coffin round the graves
till dogs howl in the darkened dawn

—all this to camoflage clandestine play
with tales at which the learned gentry smirk.
This chiaroscuro scene serves as an Emblem
—imagine it engraved in Doré's style
to illustrate an old book meant for boys
that might have caught your eye one rainy day
in 1957 in the attic
& never lost to memory since then—
a reverie so potent to evoke
it seems more real than any waking act
more full of longing than a sigh of love—
a way of knowing stronger than mere truth.

BLACK PYRAMID
(for mIEKAL aND)

I.

Some years ago in the Wisconsin pine barrens—actually the huge depression formed by the long-ago disappearance of Glacial Lake Wisconsin—somewhere around Necedah— hometown of excommunicated visionary Catholic cult with its own theme park—and the book *Wisconsin Death Trip*—strange sunken humid basin like a ghost lake thick with unbreathable air;

looking for some lost Indian Effigy Mounds, ourselves lost, car trouble, weird local people, suffocating heat. Along Country Highway "ZZ" or something, flat & straight thru deserted pines & scrub, occasional ruin of a mobile home, then tracts of bottom land & miles of caked bog;

suddenly way off to the left back amongst dwarfish pines we catch a glimpse of something—a black pyramid—maybe 20 or 25 feet high—dead black & featureless—out in the middle of nowhere—alone—no explanation—nothing.

Stop & park the car by weedy roadside—get out & walk back thru trees—no path—sweet-thorns & bugs—smell of baked putrescent vegetable matter & pines, sense of increased & measurable gravity. (Scientific query: is there in fact a measurable increase of gravity in geological depressions such as vanished lakes?)

The pyramid turns out to be a flimsy structure covered with black tarpaper, revealing cheap plywood where paper has already begun to scale away in the moist heat. The pyramid is surrounded by uncut weeds—no signs of life or occupancy. A door also covered with tarpaper is set flush into one face of the

pyramid & locked with a rusty padlock. A breathless silence prevails—
no cars are passing along the road—no birds—not even a sign of
breeze in the pines.

II.

Aleister Crowley around 1913 staged the "Rites of Eleusis" in a magical
(or magickal) chamber in London with the audience all dosed on
mescaline & morphine. He judged it a failure because stupid people
on drugs are still stupid. Like Artaud & Giordano Bruno signalling
desperately through the flames—but it's a made-for-TV movie &
no one understands them. The key is to get rid of the audience—do
theater for the spirits only.

Cornelius Agrippa hints at some kind of occult lunar telegraph
whereby messages are sent somehow via the moon. Perhaps by
dreams. The antennae could be an obelisk shaped to the mathematical
dimensions of a single moonbeam, tipped with a large moonstone or
opal, mounted on the back of a bronze sphinx,

inscribed with hieroglyph message for transmission, & left alone in
forest or desert or mountain after appropriate ritual in the style of
Marsilio Ficino with lunar correspondences—aloes, silver, absinthe,
crescent sijil, Dianic chants, etc.

An amusing & instructive incident put an end to Acèphale the
"headless" secret society founded by Bataille & Callois. In order to
transcend the trivial they demanded that one member volunteer to be
a human sacrifice. When no one stepped forward the Order had to be
disbanded.

III.
a rosicrucian gesture
a sign of distress
Count Cagliostro in a half-mask
has lost his address

locked up in our monads
like Nemo's bathysphere
je n'est pas un autre
with nothing to fear

hallucinogenic snuff
drips like green snot
the mask that Nature wears
is everything we're not.

TWO TEA TRANSLATIONS

1.

Hundred hundred feet of well stones
       thick with moss
tea brewed with such water would
       entice few guests
yet glimpsing the moon reflected
       in its midnight deeps
I might have to revise
       my low opinion.

          — "Lu Yü the Tea God
              Visits a Tea Water Well"
       Wang Yü-Chîng

2.

Reaching West Tower Temple
I found no trace of humans
where nobles once had thronged
& Master Lu Yü dwelt.
Weed encrusted halls
inhabited by frogs
& the lonely well by fish
—yet still something of
his greatness lingered.

          —Fei Shé-I
           (T'ang Dynasty)

Tombeaux

TOMBEAU FOR MALLARMÉ

In occultist circles certain books & manuscripts are sentient.
They not only intoxicate their destined readers but also poison
the destined anti-reader.

*

Manifesto of poetry as poison: this taste for flowers like lurking
around the playground.

*

Poppies, mandragore, an embarrassing Appeal to Youth or
flowers for the Dead.

TOMBEAU FOR
GÉRARD DE NERVAL

The lure of the hieroglyph lies
in the almost nauseatingly thrilling notion
that language might after all actually
communicate rather than betray us
or more precisely that the rare lightning
of telepathy via whole-body transmission
might be quintessentialized like a pill
in a rebus-heavy steganography that
de-codes itself even long after the
author is gone: text
as initiation—not ghost in machine
but afflatus in the calligramme—
perfume or mumia that will
linger even in reprints of bad translations.

A TOMBEAU FOR
GORDON CAMPBELL

Half-martyred is about the size of it: half-crazed for any
rending of any veil: the stage where wildflowers or gleams
of light on old pewter appear saturated with "your" absence.

How dispiriting: another one of those missionary tracts
written for the Vanishing Tribe of the Month Club: last
Shakers in Sabbathday Lake, last Sabbatarian Anabaptists of
Ephrata, last few readers of Swedenborg in the friggin' original.

Ecclesiastiqueens & vestment fetishists. Contrition unloosens
the tongue. Angel of automatocratic writing, angel of inkblots.
Amen. Tiny blue feather caught in fresh spiderweb by front
door: last known address.

More of the same is yer only man. More & more infinitesimal
traces, droplets on the needle's hairy molecular ultimato.
Positively byzantine, the Bishop muttered archly.

Pseudocelestial hierarchies—sort of a rogue scout troupe.
Rebel trebles. Not unlike a pipe or two of opium—including
the little touch of nausea.

There's no repetition in theophany: ya hadda be there.
Here come the Ottomans again, yawn. Sick man of Europe?
Mais, c'est moi.

The noonday demon: one is polite, masking one's fear &
arousal. Come on Verlaine, get off yr duff & sleep in a
haystack with yr rheumatism. Give the dog a bone, Arthur,
the Bear, a bottle of poire, el Cobra. Entheogenic
schwarmerei—a trembling tremendum: this is what we learned
in Fez and Damcar.

TOMBEAU FOR MANGAN
(for Robert & Charlotte)

Always at my heels I hear
James Clarence Mangan in his batwing cloak
& pointy wizard hat the taptap of his blackthorn
Georgian streets each house a decayed tooth
in a slow grimace. Culture itself
begins as a form of mourning
dust grease bones palpable ghosts
wet tweed horse sweat peatsmoke porter.
The Past is a reproach luxurious as laudanum
or ether in blueglass bottles cheaper than gin.
Modern offices & flats
haunted by buildings long erased & replaced by
spooks of boiled cabbage vanished into
long hallways of disappointed ideals
distant clipclop of aetherial pompes funèbres
wet laundry leaky drains & sooty azure
of an ectoplasmic dusk
superimposed like a cheesy
double-exposure "spirit photograph"
w/gauze oozing from the medium's ear &
taking shape as a frightened face
with the dreadful effrontery of a leper
gesticulating outside the window of a
Starbuck's or McDonald's.
A Serious Call. Standing on ladder in library
in a beam of motes hunched absorbed
over leathered annals bookstalls
in gothic galleries along greenly
odoriferous quays—tattered edition of
Aurora (1691) always just out of reach
the dark tide overwhelms us
the darkhaven.

TOMBEAU FOR MANY

(in memory of Steve Scully)

Mourning wards off haunting as witness the Victorians &
their ebony ju-ju. We use the opposite tactic. No flowers
please. Corpse avoidance—exorcism by hygiene, no grave
goods. But nothing seems to work.

Recordings once had hex power despite being essentially
dead—like gris-gris, graveyard dirt. Monk's "Tea For
Two." Harry Parch's "Hobo letter". Lovecrafts's story
about the room with the extra angle: Boolean architecture: The
Suburban Book of the Dead. The lure of heroin.

The Dead become Chinese gods gathering around like butterflies
over the offering of blood. They make appearances in
the dreams of many. They grow bigger & realer. Rumors of the new
cult reach Court, the ghosts are given titles. They dictate
their autobiographies. And so on.

The telephone is haunted as the Arabs attest. No candy
skulls, no firecrackers, no drunken fusillades, no picnics
in the graveyard.

Sometimes when you've thought many
heavy thoughts & paid for them you get
an extra thought free gratis for nothing
a rose petal floating on a full bowl
of milk, a crackerjack toy
a little plastic thought
manufactured in Taiwan,
a Bazooka Joe comic thought
a bad pun—and yet
it could be the very hinge
between creaking dimensions—the words
Sir Humphrey Davy heard when first
he inhaled his new invention
nitrous oxide: the Anesthetic Revelation.

234

IRRESPONSIBLE
FOR BRAD WILL

(murdered by P.R.I. paramilitary
Oaxaca, Oct. 27, '06)

A Christian Revenge Squad
that goes about publicly & maliciously
forgiving its enemies might at least
rise to heavy irony. Green Revenge:
take out one SUV for every acre of trees.
The bien pensant affect to despise revanchism.
Pacifists never win. Proletarian Revenge, yes,
but where are the proles when you need 'em?
Every successful bank robbery is at least a
consolation. What would be gained
by burning down the Mexican Embassy?
Well—plenty actually—and anyway
who cares? Lift a few hearts temporarily
is that nothing? Oh well—nice thought.

TOMBEAU
for Robert Anton Wilson

Poem & pomology—false etymology
or proto-Indo-European ha-ha?
The small-k kabbalist relishes
a poemogranate from the gardens of
Granada. N.E. Vavilov (later
denounced by Lysenko, died in Gulag)
discovers Eden somewhere in Khazakhstan
not far from the genetic epicenter of hemp.
Noon blue apples. The Discordian Pope
throws out the first ball of the season
over the fence into the Hesperides
or Tir na Nog the island of
Irish Facts. Turn down gents
your jiggers of Jameson's.

(an earlier version appeared
in Fifth Estate)

TOMBEAU FOR
COLIN WILSON

His philosophy of peak experience plus Walter Benjamin's Profane
Illumination equals overcoming of Nietzsche's Christ/Dionysus crisis
in the last insane letters from Turin—call it romantic existentialism
according to which one could save the phenomena of Hermeticism
as an infinite regression of skillful revelation of skillful illusion
& so on down to the putative & inexpressible but empirically
verifiable interface between consciousness & nature in the moment
of horizontal immortality which needless to say possesses political
implications.

TOMBEAU FOR LEONORA CARRINGTON

Mexico City is absolutely.
                                    Or was.
With a claridad that would've seemed
glossy as a femur except for the fecality
of its plutonian fruit. Especially
Leonora Carrington. The secret hardness
of colonial baroque. The refusal to be
reasonable. Its crown of owls.

Chocolate is Mexico's great
contribution to Surrealism.
With unbroken incantations in the
voice of a lion prepare (on wild rocks)
a soup made of half a pink onion, a bit of
perfumed wood, some grains of myrrh, a
large branch of green mint, 3 belladonna pills
covered w/ white swiss chocolate, a
huge compass rose (plunge in soup for one minute);
just before serving old Chinese "cloud" mushroom
which has snail-like antennae &
grows on owl dung.

Madame Paracelsa tells yr
fortune (in the sense of "buried treasure").
It seems you yourself have psychic gifts
which are only exacerbated by her soups.
Carrington embodies both the siesta & the
anti-siesta. A Madam Adam
with a hand cranked gramophone horn
lacquered black & gold that plays
only beeswax cylinders of Erik Satie
or Gesualdo. Here alone does exile
attain that elegance & impassibility known
only to stoned Rosicrucians.

*(Note: soup recipe by Leonora Carrington; see
The Spiritual Journey of Alejandro Jodorowsky.)*

FOOTNOTE ON A COMMENTARY ON
THE TOMBEAU FOR ANATOLE MALLARMÉ

Tower of ivory. Penetrate these dead nouns
with delicate scalpel. How many tusks.
We discovered the graveyard—killed no
narwhals or hefalumps to make
this refuge. Pull up the drawbridge
of frozen lace. The cork-lined skull of
Wanda Landowska. The spume of meerschaum.
German saints. Goldfish pagoda. Parchesi.
To live in the light of ancient teeth.
Wind reawakens the deep song of
white oceans. The pale yellow of scrimshaw.
Pull up the ladders like retractile limbs.
Let it be real as a pierced fan
that infolds itself in bone blades.

TOMBEAU FOR
GUY DAVENPORT

"as long as it doesn't frighten the horses"
a poem can be made of nothing but footnotes:
this whatchamacallit, this threnody or tombeau.
Let's spit out the gag. Nobody's
going to read this, nobody who counts.
Nobody's fishing for bicycles in the canal
& even at the time it seemed like Rasputin, immune to every
poison but one,
delicate as apple blossoming, the bitch Nostalgia.
There's no such thing as the Denmark of yr imagination
I seem to remember the ink was mauve
was it called rhodography?
Why bother to leave the house at all?—
or so we believe in the Universal Life Church
of Modesto California which for fifty dollars
made me a Bishop. "Smoke Pot, Eat Chicken, Drink Tea"
Come out. Hasten the Day.
"Data-poisoning" said the little bird—
let me sign you up for this Sun & Health Club
on some Baltic beach in 1911.
Weather fronts like vast godly thoughts from the North
pass overhead alternating with blue-gold
stretches of time which used to be filled
with aimless bicycling till that
"greatly popularized incident
in Cassel, Germany, in the 17th century...
seven doors...seven angles...seven chests...
containing
1) all our books
2) the VOCABULARIUM of Paracelsus
3) looking glasses of divers virtues, bells, burning lamps
4) chiefy wonderful artificial songs."

INSTASONNET FOR THE DEAD

Conceivably paper was invented by the Dead
first as clay which takes the lightest impression
less than a breath & only later
as pulp. The original refrigerator was
a tube thru which milk & wine were
trickled into buried coffins to refresh
thirsty ghosts & squelch their ashes
into "the first plastic" so amenable to
the shaping Imagination—so
expressive. Years after yr demise bills
still arrive & unseen liquid assets
are siphoned off into the conceptual space
of a sub-elysian afterlife—a cybersepulcher
or financial Hades of pale &
mothlike immortality.

TOMBEAU

for Lyx Ish

How can people exist without making?

Doesn't misery result from blockage of the normal human need to make?

Isn't it strange that most humans cease to make when they leave childhood?

This was not the case in most pre-industrial societies so it can
scarcely be due to Evolution can it?

Perhaps Progress?

How about this for a scenario: making is the prolongation of play not
the content of work.

Play & making constitute modes of production of meaning; "goods &
services" signify as little to the maker as wages to the playing
child.

The first gardens for example were not created to be work or even to
produce food. They were experiments in making. Love affairs with
certain meaningful plants such as hemp or grapes or tobacco.

School in the modern universal standardized institutional sense did
not exist till the industrial age. Unlike old apprenticeship systems
school teaches not making but work, or rather, it transforms the
energies of making into the bound energies of work.

The model here was mind/body as steam engine. The more you bottle up
energy, bind it & force it, the more efficient it becomes -- but also
more destitute of complexity. The less complexity, the less meaning.

Replacement of steam engine model by computer model simply speeds up
processes of machinization on psychic & physical levels:

machines take over production of meaning just as they take over
material production -- or in the case of computers, control of the
means of production (kybernetes, Greek for helmsman).

Production of meaning cannot be synthesized (rendered inorganic)
without suppression on a social level of the desire to make.

In the crude early days of industry this programme was realized thru
overt repression, control on brute physical level, fordism,
time-clock, etc.

Here in the Future however control has gone covert & non-linear. It
now operates directly on the imagination thru manipulation of
simulacra.

As A.K. Coomaraswamy said, in our modern society the artist is a
special kind of person whereas in a normal society every person is a
special kind of artist.

The specialness of the artist consists of alienation, that is, a
wound or lesion.

The artist refuses to give up playing -- the production of meaning --
and thus also refuses domestication & "socialization" -- which are
based on consumption of someone else's meaning, or rather, everyone
else's meaning: the Consensus.

The artist is seen as an incomplete person, neotenic, one who has
never grown up; thus is both despised & envied.

The artist will never be hurt, or rather, the artist is already hurt,
otherwise would not be an artist.

This reality emerges very rapidly in the late 18th century as a kind
of pre-echo of the Industrial Revolution; visionaries like Blake &
Novalis suffer as Cassandras for their foresight.

The final revenge of the average modern non-artist on the artist is
to turn art into a commodity & consume it.

In a Gift economy a made object cannot be alienated in this way, only
given or received.

Under the sign of the Gift no one "makes a living" but simply lives;
no separation between making & life.

Under the sign of money however the axe of separation cuts to the root:

money fills up with meaning while art loses it.

People feel art betrays them because it promises meaning but never delivers.

But meaning lies in making not consuming.

Only a few great connoisseurs can really appreciate art without
making it -- and in fact such appreciation is itself a kind of making.

And at some moment perhaps everyone has been a knower in this sense,
deeply moved & even changed by some art they have made their own by
understanding it,

understanding it by becoming it.

Everyone has at least one childhood memory of first-hand making.

Everyone has at least one moment of being an artist even if they're
ashamed of it.

Hobbies are often repressed art urges.

Artists who realize this dilemma can try various ways to ease the pain:

for instance by giving away their art for nothing

by teaching other people how to get over repression & make things
themselves (poesis)

by cultural sabotage -- art as negation & critique -- destruction as
creation on both conceptual & physical levels -- attack the
institutions

by keeping children out of school

by transforming work into play, e.g., by gardening in a festive &
sensual manner

by embracing wordly failure as a sign of spiritual success

by "going out to greet the sabbath", by invoking St Monday, by
slacking off, by praising revery & daydream against the slander of
utilitarians & moralists

by founding a rural commune devoted to art & avant gardening -- or

by redemption, i.e., by taking on oneself the burden of misery of the
non-artists, by being an Art Saint.

In short there are many things to do, things that might at least save
yr own sanity

from disintegration burn-out under the good-cop/bad-cop routine of
Late Late Capital

or even worse, assimilation, sell-out,

apotheosis of the Cyborg

without necessarily at the same time starving in a garret for want of
    food or recognition or even the company of friends.

Nevertheless sacrifices have to be made: one cannot simultaneously
    enjoy the conforts (however thin) of Capital & yet live as if the
    Revolution had already occured.

Some bets cannot be hedged. Play turns out to be quite serious --
    just as we suspected -- a matter of risk.

In a normal society it would take no courage to make, to create one's
    special kind of art.

Normal folk test their courage in other ways, say by vision quest, or
    by hunting dangerous game.

Like shamans artists are usually forced into it by spirits who won't
    let them rest unless they make art -- a kind of possession --

but it's always possible to appease at least some of these devils
    with a nice job in media or academia.

The result is of course self-repression & misery but many choose
    sickness with wealth over health with poverty.

In the U.S. the choice of affluence & distraction is made easy
    because the price in psychic misery is masked by false advertising &
    consciousness management.

It takes sheer foolhardiness to be an artist in the first place &
    then on top of it turn one's back deliberately on ArtWorld & retire
    to obscurity in some bohemian outback --

but the secret truth is that one year of dreamtime is worth ten of
    so-called self-appointed Real Life.

If more people knew this secret more & more people would take the
    risk until bit by bit the map would be erased
    & replaced by territory.

feb. 29 '04

LUCKY SHADOWS by Peter Lamborn Wilson
Printed in the Autonomous Republic of Qazingulaza

www.ingramcontent.com/pod-product-compliance
Lightning Source LLC
Chambersburg PA
CBHW022008100426
42736CB00041B/1035